Foreword

Of all that has to be done to make cities good to live in, nothing is more fundamental than letting in the sun and keeping open the sky. The blocked view from the window, the narrow treeless street, the pall of smoke were some of the worst effects of the lack of care and knowledge of nineteenth-century town builders. We are now beginning to get back clean air, clean water, clean streets, brighter building surfaces and, with these, more sky, cloudscape and sunshine in the urban scene. But since closely grouped buildings, to provide for the manifold activity of people at home, on business or on pleasure, are the essence of the city, we have to study how to get a maximum of sunlight and daylight in and about buildings which are close together. This is a developing science: we do a good deal better, particularly in getting daylight through our windows, than we used to, but we need to study the problem more closely. In particular, we must get sun-light to windows and into gardens of town houses and flats, especially those in close-set groups, close to the ground, of the kind we are building now. Every householder has a claim to some sun even when it rides low in the sky; and every plot that is going to be developed in the future is en-titled meanwhile to the protection of its open sky.

The Secretaries of State commend this study to planning authorities and designers and builders. It is inevitably technical but, once mastered, the procedures it suggests are not difficult and they help point the way to the better environment of the future.

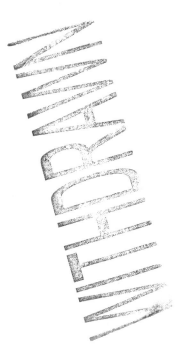

SUNLIGHT AND DAYLIGHT

PLANNING CRITERIA
AND DESIGN OF BUILDINGS

Department of the Environment
Welsh Office

London
Her Majesty's Stationery Office 1971

SBN 11 750400 9

Contents

Introduction

1

Nature and purpose of the study

1.1   This study is intended to help planning authorities and developers by setting out the aims, processes and methods of planning and designing for sunlight and daylight and by making some positive suggestions about the layout and design of buildings.

1.2   The advice given is not mandatory. The criteria put forward do not constitute a set of overriding rules. Provision for good sunlight and daylight in buildings is important but not necessarily more important than other requirements—such as the economic use of urban land, good views from windows and quiet rooms—and may sometimes be difficult to reconcile with these. In the last resort decisions must be based on common sense and judgement. This study is intended as a positive contribution to solving such problems.

1.3   Criteria for the spacing out of buildings, sometimes referred to as 'block spacing criteria,' are set out in Chapter 3. Planning authorities, when they examine proposals, can use them to safeguard sunlight and daylight in the local environment considered broadly. The architect and developer, however, are just as much concerned with another part of the process of planning and design, namely the design of individual buildings. To ensure that enough sunlight and daylight can be had inside rooms they must rely on other criteria such as those of the Codes of Practice of the British Standards Institution. Relevant sections of these codes are included in Appendix C. One of the objects of this study is to distinguish the two parts of the process and to show their relationship to each other (Chapter 4). Some design considerations, mainly to help architects and developers, are put forward in Chapter 8.

1.4   To adhere rigidly to the block spacing criteria may do more harm than good. The possibility of using an alternative set of criteria in detailed designing gives flexibility to the planning and design process. An architect may, for instance, wish to bring buildings close together to preserve a group of forest trees or maintain the character of existing development. If this involves infringement of the block spacing criterion for daylight in a difficult corner of the layout he may be able, instead, to meet the British Standards Institution's Code of Practice requirements by enlarging windows.

1.5   Similarly, to apply the block spacing criterion which protects adjoining land to the whole boundary of a site may not be appropriate. If, for instance, the development proposed is part of an overall plan which foreshadows the disposition of future buildings, consultation with owners of surrounding land and property may reveal a less onerous way of protecting their interests. Chapter 6 contains advice on this sort of case.

1.6   In short the block spacing criteria should be used with due regard to the many other factors which help to create good living conditions. They should on no account be applied rigidly as rules of thumb, but rather as a technique for ensuring that new development makes the most of its opportunities for enjoying good sunlight and daylight. If they are used discriminatingly in conjunction with other techniques in the way described in this study they will become a positive aid to good design not simply a means of negative control.

'Planning for Daylight and Sunlight'   Planning Bulletin 5 (1964)

1.7   This study completely supersedes Planning Bulletin 5 but, for those familiar with that publication, refers to it in places to show what changes are being made.

1.8   The check of block spacing by daylight and sunlight indicators as described in Planning Bulletin 5 is a well-known method which has helped to produce development in which provision for daylight, at least, is fairly good. This method is retained.

1.9   Some changes are made in the terms of advice and in the block spacing criteria put forward. Firstly, it was necessary to express dimensions in metric terms and, secondly, experience had shown a need to revise the previous criteria. The opportunity was taken to examine more closely than before the problem of designing for sunlight and also to express the new block spacing criteria for daylight more precisely and in terms which accord with present-day technical practice.

1.10   The sunlight criterion referred to in Planning Bulletin 5, involving a rather severe restriction on the designing of housing, has in practice been neglected by most planning authorities; this study sets out a new, less restrictive, criterion and advises that it should be regarded as no less important than the daylight criterion. The daylight indicators described in Planning Bulletin 5 provided a daylight criterion of block spacing more appropriate to blocks of 4 storeys or more than to close-set blocks of 2 to 4 storeys of which relatively more are now being built; for these it was over-restrictive. A new daylight criterion has therefore been devised which is more soundly based all round and particularly less restrictive for housing of this kind. The application of the new criteria will not much affect the overall density of housing development but will improve the amount of spring, summer and autumn sunlight on the faces of buildings.

1.11   The main changes made in the method of checking block spacing described in Planning Bulletin 5 can be summarised as follows.

  i More emphasis is laid on sunlight in housing layouts. For southerly faces of residential buildings the daylight criterion is abolished and replaced by a sunlight criterion. The new sunlight criterion does not, however, involve such wide spacing of buildings as the old one.

  ii The daylight criteria are modified. The new criterion for housing does not involve such wide spacing as the old one.

  iii The daylight criteria are expressed differently and more precisely in terms of the 'Sky Component'. (See Appendix B for the definition.)

  iv The sunlight and daylight indicators are re-designed to accord with the new criteria and are provided at metric scales.

Building Regulations. Rights of Light

1.12   Two matters, requiring the attention of designers but not forming part of the subject of this study, are referred to in Appendix C: first, the zone of open space requirements in Part K of the Building Regulations; second, statutory Rights of Light.

| SUNLIGHT AND DAYLIGHT | Aims of planning for sunlight and daylight | 2 |

2.1   In planning for sunlight and daylight it is essential to keep the aims in view. If this is done the question of what method to use, whether to apply block spacing criteria (Chapter 3) or some other accepted criteria (Appendix C) or simply to rely on common sense, is likely to answer itself.

2.2   These aims do not stand in isolation but form part of a set of inter-related aims with which they have to be balanced and accommodated. Thus to safeguard the close-knit character of an old town centre may in places justify closer spacing of new buildings than would normally be desirable, but this should not prevent careful design for sunlight and daylight in the detailed arrangement of open ground, walls and windows. Or, occasionally, the need may arise for a special building to provide completely controlled atmosphere, acoustical conditions and lighting, to the exclusion of sunlight and daylight altogether. Such a building may be acceptable in itself but should not be allowed to overshadow its neighbours. On the other hand, buildings in a proposed housing layout, spaced to satisfy the requirements of sunlight and daylight, may be too near to be private from each other: in housing layouts of up to three or even four storeys privacy is often the critical factor in spacing. In short the aims of planning for sunlight and daylight must be integrated with the aims of planning generally, not pressed too far, not forgotten, and not allowed to obscure other aims.

2.3   In planning specifically for sunlight and daylight the first aim is:

AIM 1

To ensure good conditions in the local environment considered broadly *with enough sunlight and daylight on and between the faces of the building blocks for good interior and exterior conditions.*

This is the main aim of planning authorities.

2.4   The second aim is:

AIM 2

To ensure in detail *that sunlight and daylight can be had just where they are wanted in particular gardens, inside particular rooms, etc.*

This is the main aim of architects and developers.

2.5   These two aims, the *general planning aim* and the *detailed designing aim,* though closely inter-related have to be distinguished. The block spacing criteria (Chapter 3) can be used in achieving the former; they are not appropriate for the latter. To realise the opportunities for detailed design presented by good block spacing, other methods and other criteria have to be used (Chapter 8, Appendix A and C).

2.6   The aims of planning for sunlight and daylight can also be described in terms of the different parts of the local environment.

Sunlight and daylight should be safeguarded:

AIM 3

within a proposed layout;

AIM 4

on land which is likely to be developed or redeveloped adjoining the proposal site;

AIM 5

in any existing building or buildings affected by the proposal.

The block spacing criteria are designed to safeguard proposed buildings and the development potential of adjoining land (AIMS 3 and 4). They are *not* designed to safeguard existing buildings (AIM 5).

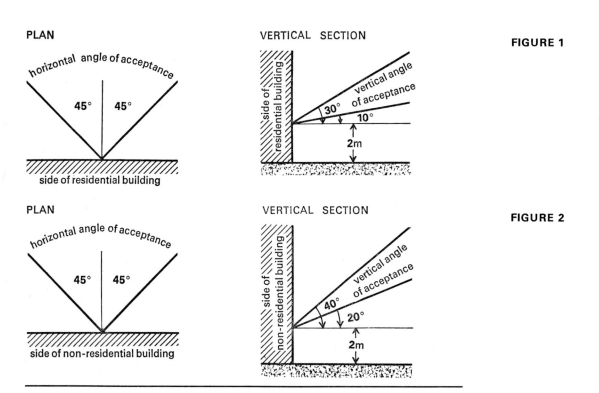

PLAN

horizontal angle of acceptance

45°   45°

side of residential building

VERTICAL SECTION

side of residential building

vertical angle of acceptance

30°   10°

2m

FIGURE 1

PLAN

horizontal angle of acceptance

45°   45°

side of non-residential building

VERTICAL SECTION

side of non-residential building

vertical angle of acceptance

40°   20°

2m

FIGURE 2

Criteria for spacing building blocks

3

3.1   This chapter contains a technical statement of the new block spacing criteria. The general description of the process of development control and design is taken up again in Chapter 4. The new criteria are introduced here because they can form the basis for an important early stage in the design process, a basis which is different in several respects from that set out in Planning Bulletin 5 (1964).

3.2.   The criteria relate to sunlight and daylight available at a low level on the sides of buildings and over boundary lines. If they are satisfied, building faces and, in most cases, the land between will be reasonably open to the available sunshine, and there will usually be enough daylight to provide good interior lighting given normal window and room dimensions; the planning authority's main aim (AIM 1) is thus likely to be achieved. However, no short set of criteria can provide a perfect safeguard of sunlighting and daylighting on and between blocks of buildings. Those that follow have to be applied with discretion. Sometimes exceptions should be allowed and sometimes other supplementary tests should be applied.

3.3   The criteria are defined with precision simply to fix unambiguous levels of reference and not because half a degree of angle or 0.1% of 'Sky Component' are significant for the quality of a layout. The fact that the levels are not expressed as round figures is simply the result of conversion from one unit of measurement ('Sky Factor') into another ('Sky Component'). (For definition of these terms see Appendix B.)

3.4   There is plenty of room for give and take in practice. The daylight indicators (7.21 to 7.34) themselves embody approximations, but they measure, near enough, whether the daylight criteria are satisfied. (The sunlight indicators, on the other hand, are precise.)

Sunlight Criterion

(southerly faces)

3.5   *Residential buildings.* In proposed buildings sides facing due south, or in any direction east or west of south (including due west), should have all points 2 metres above ground level accessible to sunlight for 3 hours on March 1. Sunlight is only counted if the sun is 10° or more above the horizon, but sunlight at a bearing of less than $22\frac{1}{2}°$ to the side of the building is *not* excluded. (The aim is to safeguard sunlighting within the proposed layout (AIM 3) as a contribution to the quality of the local environment considered broadly (AIM 1))

Daylight Criterion

(northerly faces)

3.6   *Residential buildings.* In proposed buildings sides facing due north, or in any direction east or west of north (including due east), should have, at all points 2 metres above ground level, a Sky Component of at least 0.84% between bearings of 45° to the normal and elevations of 10° and 30° upwards (figure 1). (This safeguards daylighting: again the relevant AIMS are 1 and 3.)

Daylight Criterion

3.7   *Non-residential buildings.* All sides of proposed buildings should have a Sky Component of at least 0.97% at all points 2 metres above ground level and between bearings of 45° to the normal and elevations of 20° and 40° upwards (figure 2). (This safeguards daylighting: again the relevant AIMS are 1 and 3.) This criterion, applying to the whole range of non-residential uses, is no more than a general indication and may not be appropriate in particular cases.

3.8 For the purposes of the foregoing three paragraphs, end or flank walls less than 15 metres long (as distinct from main faces) need not be considered as sides of buildings.

3.9 It may not be necessary to have sunlight for long periods on the sides of non-residential buildings. This depends on the type of building; schools may need sunlight but in lightly built offices with big windows solar heating may seriously complicate the problem of temperature control. Accordingly, no block spacing criterion based on sunlight is put forward. It should not be forgotten, however, that sitting-out places in sunshine at midday between May and September are highly valued by city workers.

3.10 *Plot boundaries.* If land adjoining or across the road from a proposed building development of any kind needs to be protected for foreseeable *residential* building development, the common boundary should have, at all points 2 metres above ground level, a Sky Component of at least 4.30% inwards over the site of the proposed building between bearings of 65° to the normal and elevations of 19° 26′ and 49° 6′ (figure 3). (The aim is to safeguard the potential daylighting of adjoining land (AIM 4) as a contribution to the quality of the local environment considered broadly (AIM 1). To avoid complexity a criterion to safeguard sunlight on adjoining land is not included.)

Boundary Criterion

PLAN

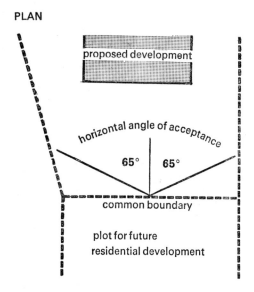

VERTICAL SECTION

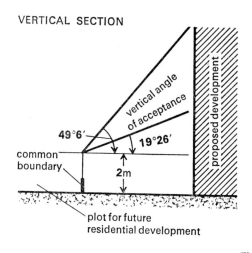

FIGURE 3

3.11 *Plot boundaries.* If land adjoining or across the road from a proposed building development of any kind needs to be protected for foreseeable *non-residential* building development, the common boundary should have, at all points 2 metres above ground level, inwards over the proposed building, a Sky Component of at least 2.90% between bearings of 65° from the normal and elevations of 36° 3′ and 59° 13′ upwards (figure 4).
(This safeguards daylighting: again the relevant AIMS are 1 and 4. To avoid complexity a criterion to safeguard sunlight on adjoining land is not included.)

Boundary Criterion

3.12 For the purposes of the foregoing two paragraphs the centre line of any road between two plots may be counted as the boundary.

3.13 For the purposes of the sunlight and daylight criteria (3.5 to 3.7) obstructions outside (as well as inside) the proposal site—any buildings that exist and are likely to remain and any to be constructed in the near future—should be taken into account. For the purposes of the boundary criteria (3.10, 3.11), however, only the development inside the proposal site should be taken into account.

PLAN

VERTICAL SECTION

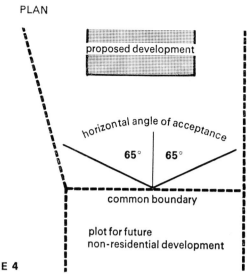

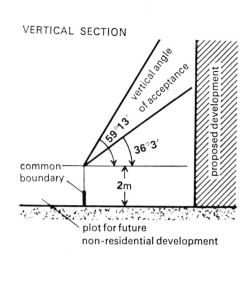

proposed development

horizontal angle of acceptance

65° 65°

common boundary

plot for future
non-residential development

vertical angle
of acceptance

59°13′

36°3′

common
boundary

2m

plot for future
non-residential development

FIGURE 4

3.14 The two criteria for residential buildings (3.5 and 3.6) may be reversed in the case of a building with sides facing in the general directions east and west: the sunlight criterion (3.5) may be applied to the side facing due east or slightly north of east or north of west and the daylight criterion (3.6) to the other side; but if this is done a study should be made of the extent and duration of shadow on the ground (3.19.ii).

3.15 Since these criteria relate to block spacing they should be applied to *generalised* outlines of buildings (figure 5) and to similarly generalised boundary lines. Roofs should be taken as flat and projections and re-entrants from building faces ignored. Details of building form, though not to be considered at this stage, do seriously affect conditions in particular rooms and open places: they need to be considered at the stage of detailed design (8.28 to 8.33, 7.13).

3.16 These criteria all apply at a level of 2 metres above the ground because this normally corresponds to the top part of the ground floor windows. It is usually at this level that light from the sky can penetrate deeply into the ground floor of the building (figure 6). Some cases in which this 2-metre level is not appropriate are referred to in paragraph 4.14.

3.17 Satisfaction of the criteria facilitates the achievement of AIM 2 (good detailed design) but does not ensure it. In particular it does not ensure that adequate sunlight and daylight will always penetrate far enough inside rooms; that will largely depend on the use of the room in question and the light needed for that use, on the size and shape of the room, and on the height and width of the windows. One can see the effect of the height of a window in figure 6: a lower window head would cut off much of the visible sky. The appropriate criteria for daylight inside rooms are those set out in the British Standards Institution's Code of Practice (C5, C6).

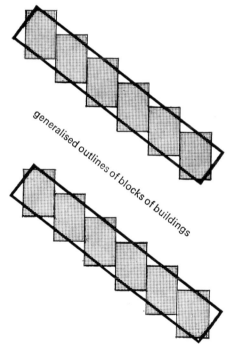

generalised outlines of blocks of buildings

FIGURE 5

3.18 The block spacing criteria should not be applied in estimating the effects of proposals on existing buildings, for instance in estimating whether a particular house will be deprived of too much light by an extension next door: this cannot be judged without reference to detail (6.1 to 6.5).

3.19 Two particular cases in which the block spacing criteria are not adequate for planning purposes and which the planning authorities should always look at carefully, and if necessary apply other tests, are:

i complex building forms (4.15);

ii spaces, enclosed or partly enclosed by buildings, without gaps on the south and therefore having extensive shadow on the ground (4.16).

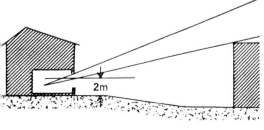

2m

FIGURE 6

3.20   One shortcoming of these criteria is that they do not take account of light reflected from the ground or from other buildings. Planning authorities should bear in mind that reflective surfaces (e.g. light gravel ground and whitewashed walls) may to some extent compensate for inadequate light directly from the sky.

Sunlight and daylight in development control

4

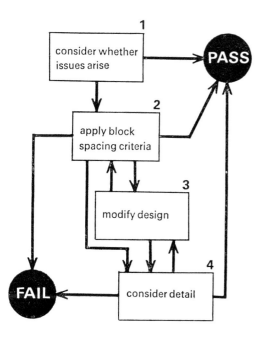

FIGURE 7

4.1 The following paragraphs show how planning authorities considering applications for development may use the block spacing criteria and, if necessary, other aids to design in a stage-by-stage process. Some cases will raise no issue of sunlight and daylight, or issues that are easily decided; others may need deeper examination. Four stages can be distinguished in the full process.

Stage 1 Consider whether any issues of planning for sunlight and daylight arise.

Stage 2 Apply block spacing criteria.

Stage 3 Modify block spacing design.

Stage 4 Consider detail.

Full consideration involving all the stages may not often be necessary. The process is illustrated in the flow chart (figure 7).

Stage 1 Consider whether any planning issues arise

4.2 At this stage the planning authority consider whether the proposal is going to have any serious effect at all on sunlighting and daylighting of the environment considered broadly. Proposals for single houses standing by themselves or filling a small gap in a terrace, for example, might be seen to have no general effect on the locality: the planning authority would then be able to decide straight away that no issue of sunlight and daylight arose and clear the proposals from this point of view without applying the block spacing criteria.

4.3 On the other hand sunlight and daylight issues are almost always raised by, for example, a large new building in a town or a considerable group of housing whether in town or country. The former would probably affect surrounding land and property. The latter, even if isolated, would form its own local environment. In both cases the planning authority would probably have to decide that clearance of the proposal was not possible without further examination (in Stage 2).

4.4 There will be borderline cases. In the last resort the question of whether planning issues are raised, whether the sunlight and daylight of the local environment considered broadly are going to be affected, is a matter of judgement.

Stage 2 Apply block spacing criteria

4.5 If it appears that the proposal does raise 'planning issues,' the next step is to apply the block spacing criteria, using either the indicators or some other method of measurement. The use of the indicators is described in detail in Chapter 7.

4.6 If the appropriate criteria are satisfied for all sides of buildings, and all relevant parts of the boundary of the plot, the application may normally be cleared from the point of view of sunlight and daylight. (Exceptional cases which may need further scrutiny are mentioned in paragraphs 3.19, 4.15 and 4.16.)

4.7 On the other hand the layout may fail to satisfy the criteria so extensively and seriously as to warrant outright refusal of planning permission.

4.8 Between the obvious passes and the obvious failures will be cases which deserve special consideration although they do not entirely satisfy the criteria. Such layouts may be well and closely designed to meet special needs. A planning authority should however require the applicant to justify such a design convincingly before clearing it in respect of sunlight and daylight.

4.9 Finally there will be cases where the areas of the layout which fail to satisfy the criteria are not extensive and where the remedy lies in asking the applicant to improve the design (Stage 3).

Stage 3   Modify block spacing design

4.10 This modification, which may be carried out by the applicant, by himself or in collaboration with the planning authority, will involve improving provision for sunlight and daylight, by elimination of buildings or parts of buildings which do not satisfy or prevent satisfaction of the criteria, and replacement with new buildings or raised levels of buildings elsewhere, by re-orientation of blocks more towards the sun, by the open-up of layouts to sunlight on the south side, and so on. The new design must then again be tested by the criteria as in Stage 2.

Stage 4   Consider detail

4.11 If AIM 1, good conditions in the environment considered broadly, is achieved, the planning authority will in general be able to leave the achievement of good conditions in detail (AIM 2) to the architect and developer and not use their development control powers for the purpose. In some cases, however, they will find that broad consideration is not enough and will need to proceed to Stage 4.

4.12 Thus detail may need to be considered as a direct result of the Stage 2 examination which may have shown up certain areas of layout as failing to satisfy the block spacing criteria. The applicant may claim that these areas have been designed in detail so that the apparent inadequacies of sunlight and daylight provision have been allowed for or compensated for. He may, for instance, have introduced windows in end walls where the criteria are not applicable (3.8) or avoided having ground floor living rooms in the area of failure, or made the rooms shallow to bring more of the floor area within range of penetration of adequate daylight, or he may have got more daylight and sunlight by having tall windows. His claim must be examined and if necessary tested. If, in particular, he arranges to meet the current standards of daylight set by the British Standards Institution (Appendix C) by such means rather than by spacing out buildings, he should not be prevented from doing so. He is entitled to show by accepted methods of measurement (Appendix A) that daylight inside rooms is up to these standards.

4.13 If, however, parts of a layout which do not satisfy the block spacing criteria are tested by detailed criteria, such as those of the British Standards Institution's Codes of Practice, it should not be forgotten that sunlight in spaces outside buildings is important. This is not at present (1971) fully

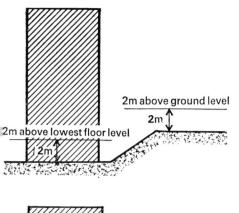

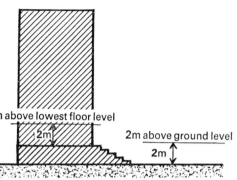

FIGURE 8

considered by the Codes of Practice. It may therefore be necessary to test the incidence of sunlight and shadow at selected points in the open between buildings (8.6 to 8.10).

4.14   Often the relation of the base of the building to ground level may need detailed consideration. A block with windows in a basement will need to be spaced further from an opposite parallel block than a normal application of the criteria would allow, but a block in which the lowest floor rooms open on to steps above the ground may need less space than the criteria would require. In such cases the appropriate block spacing criteria may be applied at a level of 2 metres above the base of the lowest storey rather than above ground level (figure 8).

4.15   Again detail may need to be considered in cases mentioned above (3.19) where the block spacing criteria are not a good enough test. One such case is that of the complex building block. A cluster of juxtaposed patio houses, for instance, is not adequately tested by applying block spacing criteria to the outlines of the cluster. One needs to know also whether provision of sunlight and daylight in a typical house within the cluster is adequate, to what extent, for instance, sun on March 1 will reach the living room windows of the patio, and what measure of daylight can be expected at reference points inside the living room. Similarly the internal arrangement of blocks of flats containing single-aspect dwellings should be checked to ensure that provision for sunlight and daylight in typical individual dwellings is sufficient.

4.16   A second such case in which the block spacing criteria may need to be supplemented by detailed consideration is the court enclosed by buildings on three or four sides with no opening on the south (figure 14). The planning authority may need to assess not only sunlight on the sides of the buildings but also the shadow on the ground. If the uses of the court require sunlight, an opening on the south may be necessary (8.8).

4.17   In special cases the planning authority may wish to examine in detail proposals which satisfy the criteria of block spacing, but in which the design of buildings is bad from the point of view of sunlight or daylight. The main rooms of a dwelling may have an unattractive, sunless view towards the north; balconies or projecting kitchens and garages may reduce the effective visibility of sky and sun to much below desirable standards. Normally decisions on planning applications should depend less on the detailed design of proposed buildings than on their general relationship to each other and to their setting. The detailed design is essentially a matter between a designer and his client. But the planning authority are concerned to see that detailed design does not stultify block spacing, and should always be ready to advise the applicant how to make good use of the potential sunlight and daylight that adequate spacing provides. A council will certainly want to ensure that their own housing is well designed in detail.

4.18   Consideration of detail may lead either to a pass or a fail of the application or to changes in design and further detailed consideration of the modified scheme.

4.19   Illustrations of the stages in development control outlined above are given in figures 9 to 12.

4.20   Chapter 8 of this study reverts to the subject of detailed design.

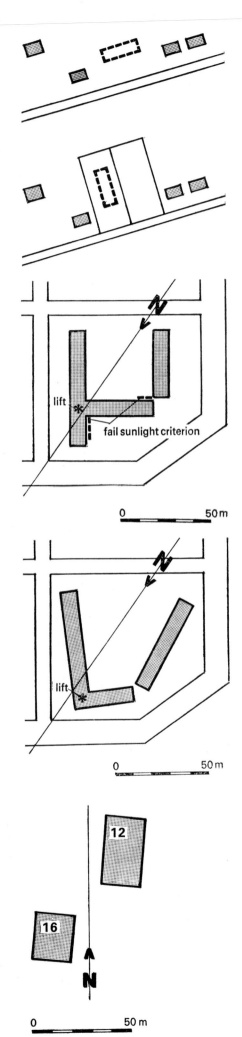

FIGURE 9

Stage 1   Do any issues arise in planning for sunlight and daylight?

An environment of scattered dwellings along a road may still have the same sunlight and daylight characteristics if a terrace of houses is added. If so, the application may be cleared from this point of view as raising no planning issues. If, however, the proposal is to build the terrace perpendicular to the road and the adjoining plot is also serviced building land, the issue is raised of safeguarding development potential. The block spacing boundary criterion should be applied to the common boundary of the two plots (Stage 2).

FIGURE 10

Stage 2 Apply block spacing criteria.

6-storey deck access blocks.
Latitude 51°N. 16.0m above ground level; 14.0m above 2m level. Daylight block spacing criteria for sides of buildings and boundaries (street centre lines) are satisfied. The sunlight criterion is not satisfied at the places shown.

FIGURE 11

Stage 3   Modify design of block spacing.

The design of the previous layout is modified by eliminating the projection on the north-west and opening the 3 sided-court towards the sun.
Total amount of building is the same. The block spacing criteria are now satisfied.

FIGURE 12

Stage 4   Consider detail.

A 16-storey tower block to the south-west of a 12-storey block. This layout satisfies the block spacing criteria but one must look at detail because the 12-storey block is likely to have single aspect flats facing west which would be overshadowed by the 16-storey block. The latitude of the place is 53°N.
As designed, the 12-storey block has in fact six flats per floor. Of the flats on the west side only the kitchen window of the southernmost flats can receive 3 hours of sunlight on March 1 on all storeys. The living room window of the southernmost flats will not satisfy the criterion on any storey. That of the nor-thernmost flats will satisfy above 7 storeys and that of the flats between, above 10 storeys.
The simplest way to overcome this serious deprivation of sunlight would be to locate the 16-storey block due south of the 12-storey block where it would overshadow only kitchen windows.

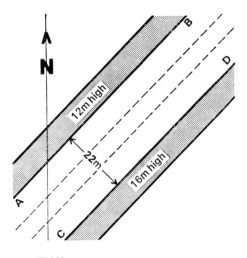

lat.: 55° N

FIGURE 13

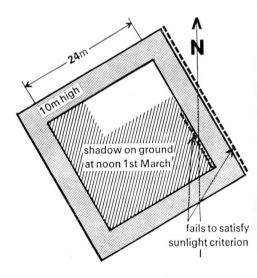

lat.: 53°N

FIGURE 14

Practical consequences of the block spacing criteria

5

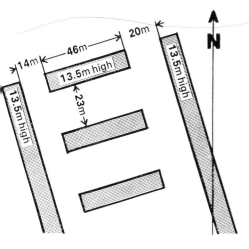

at.:51°N

FIGURE 15

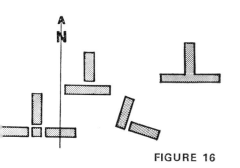

FIGURE 16

Residential buildings

5.1   Hitherto the daylight criterion for the spacing of residential buildings has usually been regarded as more important than the sunlight criterion: from now on the sunlight criterion should receive equal attention. As has been said already this will generally not involve greater costs or lower densities, since the two new criteria are individually less restrictive than those they replace; but it will generally improve the amount of spring, autumn and summer sunlight on the faces of buildings. Figures 13 to 15 illustrate the effect of the new criteria.

5.2.   In figure 13 a road running north-east and south-west has indefinitely long residential terraces on each side. The spacing shown in figure 13 satisfies the new block spacing criteria but would not have satisfied the old sunlight and daylight indicators. The new sunlight criterion, which is the operative one for testing the face AB, permits higher building across the road than the old daylight indicators would have done at the same spacing (for this particular case, and with this orientation, half as high again). The new daylight criterion which is the operative one for testing the face CD also permits a higher building opposite (about 2 metres higher) than the old daylight indicators would have done at the same spacing.

5.3   Figure 14 shows a closed residential square which satisfies the old daylight indicators and the new daylight criterion but fails to give access to three hours of sunlight on March 1, at the 2-metre level, on any one complete face of the north-eastern block of the building. Had this square been turned slightly clockwise the sunlight criterion would have been satisfied on the east face (3.14), but the problem of shadow on the ground inside the square would still have required special consideration (4.16).

5.4   Figure 15 shows a layout of 'opposed' blocks which satisfies the new criteria. It satisfies neither the old daylight nor the old sunlight indicators.

5.5.   The commonest form of failure to provide for adequate sun in layout is a juxtaposition of blocks illustrated in figure 16: the blocks or projections on the south place part of the buildings on the north in lasting shadow.

Non-residential buildings

5.6   The non-residential block spacing criteria are based on daylight alone and are not very different in their effect from those of Planning Bulletin 5 (1964). They allow long parallel buildings less than 18 metres high to be slightly closer together but require higher buildings of this form to be slightly further apart.

Miscellaneous points

6

Protection of existing buildings

6.1   One of the aims of planning for sunlight and daylight is to protect existing buildings (AIM 5, 2.6); but interested parties cannot automatically expect that any proposed buildings should stand clear to the extent indicated by the block spacing criteria.

6.2   The sunlighting and daylighting of an existing building depend not only on its freedom from obstruction by other buildings but also on its own orientation, fenestration and internal room arrangements. One therefore cannot assess the effect of adding to the external obstructions without taking all these factors into account. The protection of an existing building should be based on an assessment of what difference the proposal would make to it, i.e. to a comparison of 'before' and 'after' conditions at important places such as (in the case of a house) the interior of the living room or kitchen or on the lawn.

6.3   This 'before' and 'after' assessment can often be made by an expert on-site judgement without measurement. If measurement of daylight is necessary the daylight indicators should *not* be used. The appropriate methods, which measure the 'Daylight Factor' inside rooms, are described in Appendix A. (The term 'Daylight Factor' is defined in Appendix B). The appropriate sunlight indicator can be used to assess conditions on March 1 —the duration of potential sunlight at particular points or the extent of shadows outside the building. To measure the likely loss of sunlight at other times of the year, in summer or winter, instruments or specially constructed indicators can be used (Appendix A).

6.4   Other considerations relevant to the question of whether and how far existing buildings should be protected will be the functional efficiency, value and likely life of the building in question, and in particular whether it is listed as being of historic or architectural value. One must also consider whether it is itself a good neighbour, standing back from the boundaries of its plot and taking only its fair share of sunlight and daylight.

6.5   A common form of the 'existing building' problem faced by planning authorities is whether to allow extensions such as the building of a kitchen, or a room above the kitchen, to which owners or occupiers of neighbouring existing houses may object. Often in the past planning authorities have mistakenly sought to apply daylight indicators in these sorts of cases. They occur so often that some planning authorities may find it helpful, in the light of experience and the advice given in this and other publications, to formulate a development control policy as a guide to particular decisions, and possibly to incorporate the policy in their Development Plan.

Protection of adjoining land

6.6   Protection of 'adjoining land' (Aim 4, 2.6) is the purpose of the plot boundary criteria (3.10 and 3.11). This protection does not have to be given automatically to all surrounding land but only to land where development or redevelopment can be foreseen.

6.7   If development can be foreseen the decision whether to apply the criterion strictly may still depend on the length of time likely to elapse before development occurs and also on the extent and importance of that development. A judgement may also be needed about the form the development is likely to take: it is clearly unnecessary to require a building which presents a flank wall without windows to its plot boundary to be set back from that boundary if future development on the other side is also likely to present a flank wall without windows.

Sunlight and daylight indicators

7

General

7.1   Sunlight and daylight indicators are well known in planning offices. As they can be used quickly and conveniently, are inexpensive and easily reproduced, they are likely to remain in regular use. They should not, however, be regarded as constituting the block spacing criteria. These criteria have been defined independently in Chapter 3 and one may use any reliable method of determining whether they are satisfied. The indicators are one method of checking sunlight and daylight conditions; other methods, some of them more precise and comprehensive, are available if required (Appendix A).

7.2   The packet of indicators is published separately. It contains 21 transparencies. Nine of these are March 1 sunlight indicators for each of three latitudes, 51° (southern, marked S), 53° (central, marked M), 55° (northern, marked N), and three metric scales, 1:1250, 1:500 and 1:200. On the other twelve transparencies are daylight indicators of 4 kinds (A, B, C and D) for the same three metric scales. The price of the packet is £2.50. Planning authorities may need to keep readily available only those sunlight indicators which relate to the latitude of their own areas.

Sunlight indicators: general

7.3   One purpose of sunlight indicators is to estimate, for any point in a layout plan, the length of time for which the sun will be visible (on a clear day) round the side or over the top of buildings and other obstacles. In particular they enable one to find out whether the block spacing criterion (3.5 and 3.14) is satisfied.

7.4   A second purpose is to show where shadows of buildings and other obstacles in the layout will fall at any time and, in particularly, the extent of shadow in courts and patios, roof terraces, etc. (3.9, 3.19, 4.16, 5.3, 6.3 and Chapter 8).

7.5   The apparent path of the sun in the sky depends on the latitude of the place from which it is seen and on the time of year. Consequently sunlight indicators are different in different latitudes and different seasons. (Those in the published packet are for one season, March 1, only, but others can be constructed—see Appendix A). Also they have to be at the scale of the plan. One must therefore be sure to use the right sunlight indicator.

7.6   For measurement, by whatever means, of potential sunlight and shadow, orientation must be known. The north–south direction should therefore be marked accurately by a line running right across the plan one is using. A rough indication by means of a north point symbol is inadequate. National Grid lines are shown on all post-war Ordnance Survey maps. For ordinary measurements these are close enough to true north–south and east–west; for complete accuracy one may apply the corrections set out at the base (of 1 inch, 2½ inch and 6 inch to the mile or new metric 1:10,000 Ordnance Survey sheets) or one may use the indications in the margins to draw lines of longitude across the map.

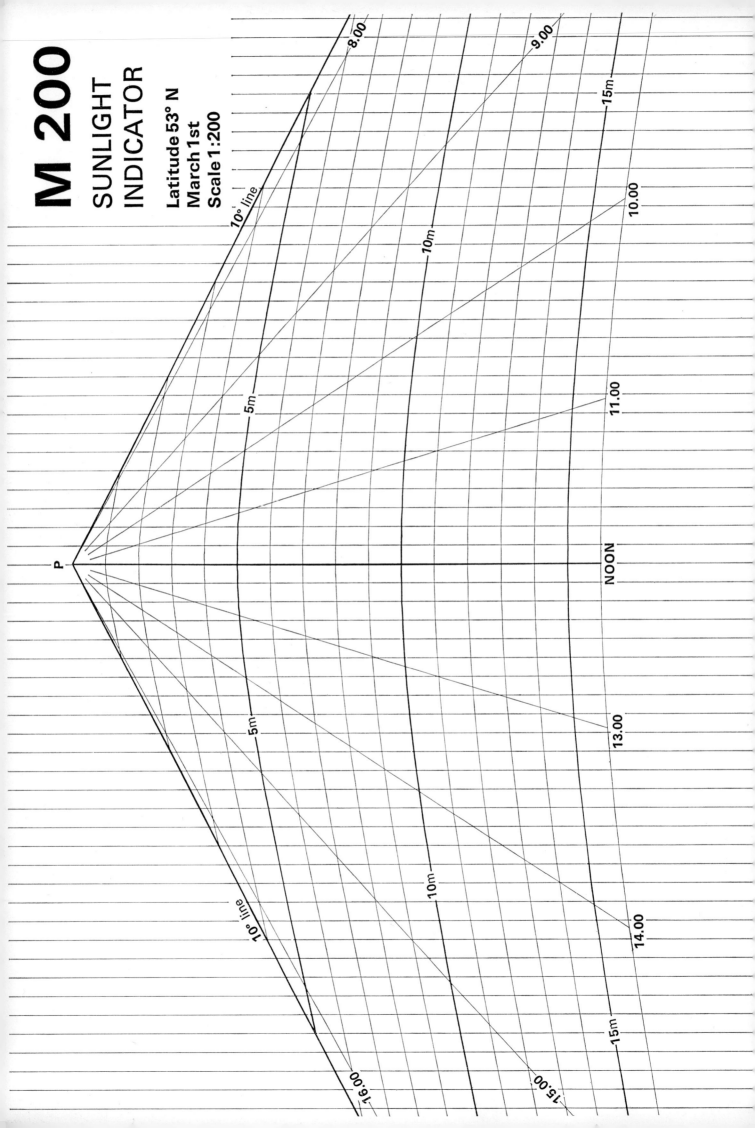

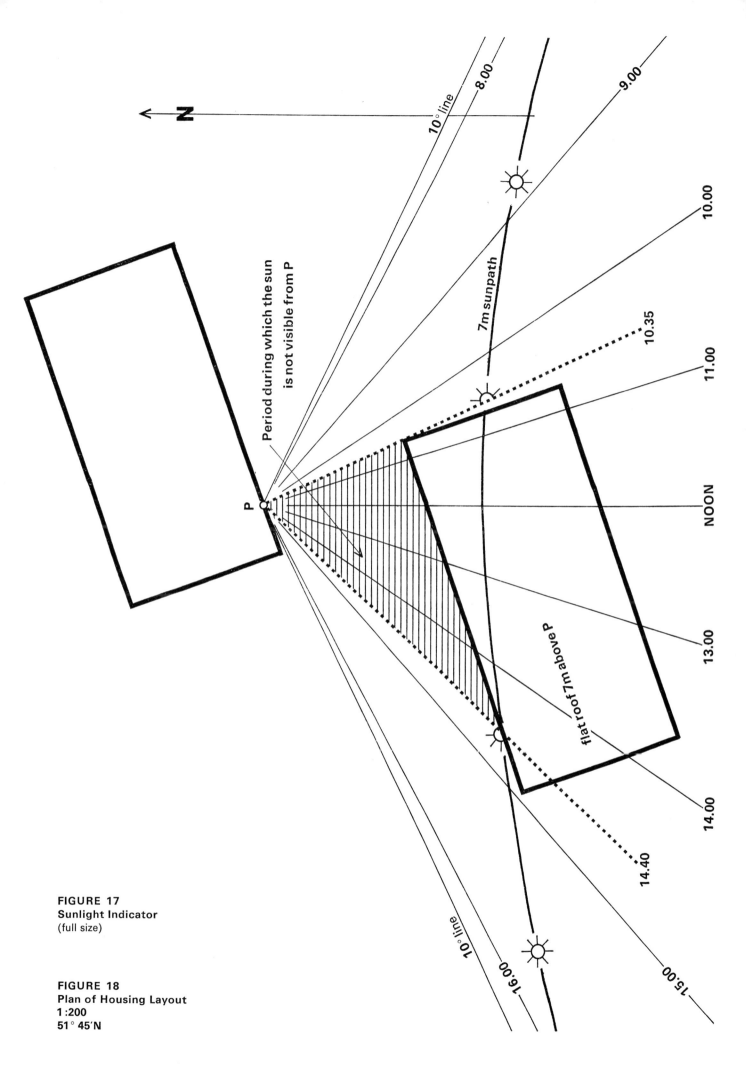

FIGURE 17
Sunlight Indicator
(full size)

FIGURE 18
Plan of Housing Layout
1:200
51° 45′N

N

10° line
8.00
9.00
10.00
7m sunpath
10.35
11.00
NOON
13.00
14.00
14.40
15.00
16.00
10° line

Period during which the sun is not visible from P

P

flat roof 7m above P

Sunlight indicators: sunlight measurement

7.7 Each of the curves on a sunlight indicator can be regarded as a 'sun-path' projected on to a horizontal plane surface. Thus in figure 17, which is a print of a 1:200 scale, sunlight indicator, the fifth curve out from P is the sunpath in relation to a plane 5 metres above P, and so on. In other words for an observer at P, the sun will appear to move along the sun-path in the plane he is considering. The time of the passage of the sun at any point on its path can be judged in relation to the radial 'hour lines' marked 8.00, 9.00 and so on to 16.00

7.8. Suppose one wants to know how long a point P in a housing layout (figure 18) will be in the sun on March 1, assuming the sky to be clear. One should proceed as follows.
 i Select the sunlight indicator appropriate to the latitude of the place (southern England) and the scale of the plan (1:200).
 ii Set the indicator on the plan with the vertex P on the point P in the layout.
 iii Orientate the indicator so that the line from P to 'NOON' runs due south from P (since the sun will be due south at noon).
 iv Select the appropriate sunpath. (In this layout there is only one obstacle, a building with a flat roof 7 metres above P. Attention has therefore to be fixed on the 7-metre horizontal plane through the roof and the 7-metre sunpath related to it.)
 v Note the times the sun goes behind obstacles and comes out from them.

7.9 The application of the sunlight indicator in this case shows that, at the point P, the sun is visible from early morning when it attains 10° altitude (off the edge of the plan) until about 10.35 hours. At about 10.35 it disappears round the side of the building, remaining obscured until about 14.40 hours. It then reappears over the roof line and remains visible for the rest of the day. Thus between the limits of the '10° lines', during which sunlight is counted for the purposes of the criterion, the sun is visible from P on a clear day for about $4\frac{1}{4}$ hours, and is obscured for just over 4 hours.

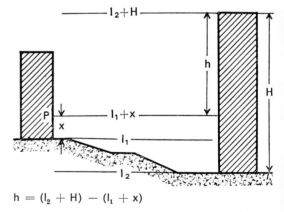

7.10 The operation described in paragraph 7.9 can be carried out from a point P at any level: the potential sunlight can be tested for example at second floor or third floor window level, but in each case the *relative* height of the obstacle above the chosen level must be known so that the appropriate sunpath line on the indicator can be selected. If the point P is x above its ground level l_1 its total height will be $l_1 + x$. Similarly if the height of the obstacle is H above its ground level l_2 its total height is $l_2 + H$ (see figure 19). The required relative height h is the difference of these totals:
$h = (l_2 + H) - (l_1 + x)$.
This holds true whichever ground level is higher (figure 19).

7.11 The block spacing criteria relate to points on the face of the building 2 metres above ground level at the foot of the building, i.e. x = 2m. The operative relative height (in metres) for the purposes of the criteria is therefore given by:
$h = (l_2 + H) - (l_1 + 2)$
or, if the ground is level i.e. $l_1 = l_2$,
$h = H - 2$.
Sometimes, however, as explained in paragraph 4.14, one may need to consider the buildings in detail and test points higher or lower than 2 metres up the face of the building.

7.12 Often several obstructions may occur in the field of view from the point being tested. Each must be considered separately. If, for example, in figure 18 the plan showed another building to the east of P, rising to a height of 8 metres relative to P then, using the same sunlight indicator in the same position and following the 8-metre sunpath, the times of obscuration would be noted for that building in the same way as before. The total

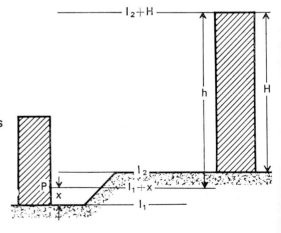

FIGURE 19

time of obscuration would then be composed of those for each building. In testing a complex layout several sunpath lines may have to be followed corresponding to the several heights of obstructions. In practice the height of each obstruction relative to P should be pencilled on the plan before the test is made.

7.13 Sometimes an obstruction has a complicated outline. Thus in figure 18 the building, instead of having a flat roof, may have a roof which slopes either way from a central ridge 8½ metres above P. Estimating the sunpath for 8½ metres by interpolation between those for 8 metres and 9 metres on the sunlight indicator one finds that the ridge would obscure the sun from about 10.40 hours to about 12.30 hours. Since the obstruction due to the flat roof is from 10.35 to 14.40 (7.9) the addition of a ridge in this case makes no difference to the sunlight at P: the effective obstruction would be at eaves level. In many cases however, the ridge, not the eaves, is the effective obstruction, and in some cases the sun may first be obscured by the eaves and reappear over the ridge or vice versa. In short an obstruction with a complicated outline may need to be considered at more than one level.

7.14 The point P to be tested may be on the side of a building facing some direction more easterly or westerly than southerly. If so some sunshine will be lost irrespective of whether the view is obstructed or not: the sun will be behind the face of the building itself for a part of its course. Thus if the building faces due west the 'NOON' line of the sunlight indicator coincides with the face of the building and sunlight can shine on this face only after noon for just over 4 hours (at over 10° elevation). The hours corresponding to any part of the sunlight indicator which lies behind the face of the building being tested must be excluded: this applies right up to the corner of the building. Figure 20 shows a case in which the hours from about 13.40 must be excluded.

7.15 To apply the sunlight criterion to a layout one must first decide (in the light of paragraphs 3.5 and 3.14) which sides of buildings are to be tested. One must then test points 2 metres up which appear to be most overshadowed, namely those having obstructions well over 2 metres high which will be intersected by the 'fan' of the indicator opened towards the south. Experience will enable one to limit the testing often to only a few critical points in the layout. The test is applied to generalised building forms (3.15).

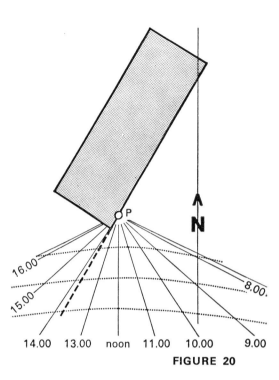

FIGURE 20

Sunlight indicators: shadow measurement

7.16 The tip of the shadow of, say, a vertical pole traces out a 'shadow path' on the ground below, moving from the west at dawn to the east at sunset and passing to the north of the pole at midday. The sunlight indicators can be used to determine the position of such a shadow. To measure shadows sunlight indicators must be oriented due *north*, that is in the opposite direction from their orientation in sunlight measurement. Each of the curves on a sunlight indicator can, for this purpose, be regarded not as a sunpath but as a 'shadow path.' Thus taking figure 17 again, the fourth curve out from P is the shadow path on March 1 (October 15) of a salient point on a horizontal plane 4 metres below it; the fifth curve is the shadow path 5 metres below it and so on. The time of the passage of the shadow at any point on its path can be judged in relation to the radial hour lines.

7.17 The shape of the shadow of a building can be estimated from the position of the shadows of one or more of its salient points.

7.18 Figure 21 illustrates the application of the indicator to show the extent of shadow at noon on March 1 in a residential court 40 metres square, surrounded by buildings 15 metres high, situated in a town on latitude 54° 30'. In this case the 1:1250 indicator for northern England is

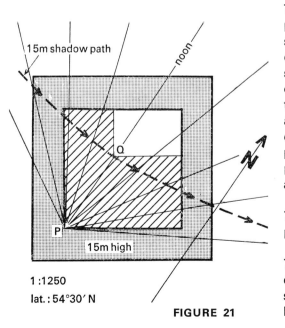

1:1250

lat.: 54°30' N

FIGURE 21

selected and applied to the southern corner of the court with the 'NOON' line running due *north* from P. The 15-metre 'shadow path' intersects the 'NOON' line at the position Q of the shadow of P. From Q the shadows of the roof lines run parallel to the sides of the court.

7.19   Figure 22 shows the extent to which, for a given latitude, season and time of day, a row of houses overshadows adjoining gardens. In this sort of case one must estimate which will be the salient points casting shadows (A, B, C and the end of the roof ridge F) and determine the shadow of each by the procedure described above.

7.20   The sunlight indicators in the published packet are for March 1. One may, however, need to determine how shadows fall in the summer months when people are more likely to sit in the open. Ways of doing this are given in Appendix A. (See also 8.6 to 8.10.)

Daylight indicators

7.21   The purpose of the daylight indicators is to test whether or not buildings satisfy the appropriate block spacing criteria (3.6, 3.7, 3.10, 3.11). This they do with reasonable accuracy though not with complete precision. It is not their purpose to measure the Sky Component available but simply to provide a 'yes' or 'no' answer to the question 'does the point being tested achieve the Sky Component specified in the criterion?' If a measure of the Sky Component is required one of the methods in Appendix A may be used.

7.22   Daylight indicators of the same kind as those published with this study have been in use since 1947, and those which were in use between 1964 and 1971 were fully described in Planning Bulletin 5 (1964). The method remains essentially the same. The following paragraphs describe the new indicators, illustrate their use and point out the innovations.

7.23   The total number of transparencies containing daylight indicators in the published packet is twelve, a reduction from the sixteen previously in use. The reduction is achieved by having only three, instead of four, indicators in each of the sets A, B, C, D, and putting all three, instead of only two, on a transparency. There are thus four transparencies at each of three scales (1:1250, 1:500 and 1:200).

7.24   No change has been made in the significance of the sets A, B, C and D. The D and C sets are 'building to building' indicators applied to sides of buildings, D to residential proposals and C to non-residential proposals. The B and A sets are 'boundary' indicators applied to boundaries and street centre lines to protect the development potential of adjoining land, B where this potential is residential and A where it is non-residential. For all 4 sets of indicators the point of application is usually taken as being 2 metres above ground level: the heights indicated on the arcs are *relative to this point* whatever its height. (Figure 19 and 7.10 and 7.11 apply to daylight as to sunlight indicators).

7.25   Figure 23 is a print of the 1:200 scale transparency containing indicators D1, D2 and D3 which are those applicable to the sides of proposed residential buildings in the plan of any proposal. The arcs in the indicators show the restriction on the height and the nearness of obstructions, and the central angle shows the horizontal sweep over which the restriction applies. The D1 indicator imposes a mild restriction on the height and nearness of obstructions on a wide front—90° of horizontal angle. The D3 indicator, on the other hand, imposes a very severe restriction on height and nearness—obstructions of the same height must be three times as far away, but it applies this only over a narrow front—18.6° of horizontal angle. D2 imposes a medium restriction over a medium front—45° of horizontal angle.

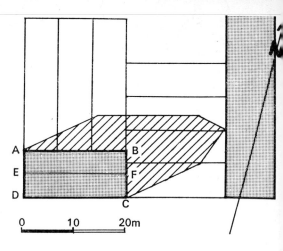

March 1st	level ground
lat.: 52°N	eaves: 5m
time: 15.00	ridge: 6.5m

FIGURE 22

FIGURE 23
Daylight Indicator
(full size)

D 200

DAYLIGHT INDICATOR

**Residential
Building to
building
Scale 1:200**

Reminder:
2m must usually be added
to give permissible height
of blocks above ground level

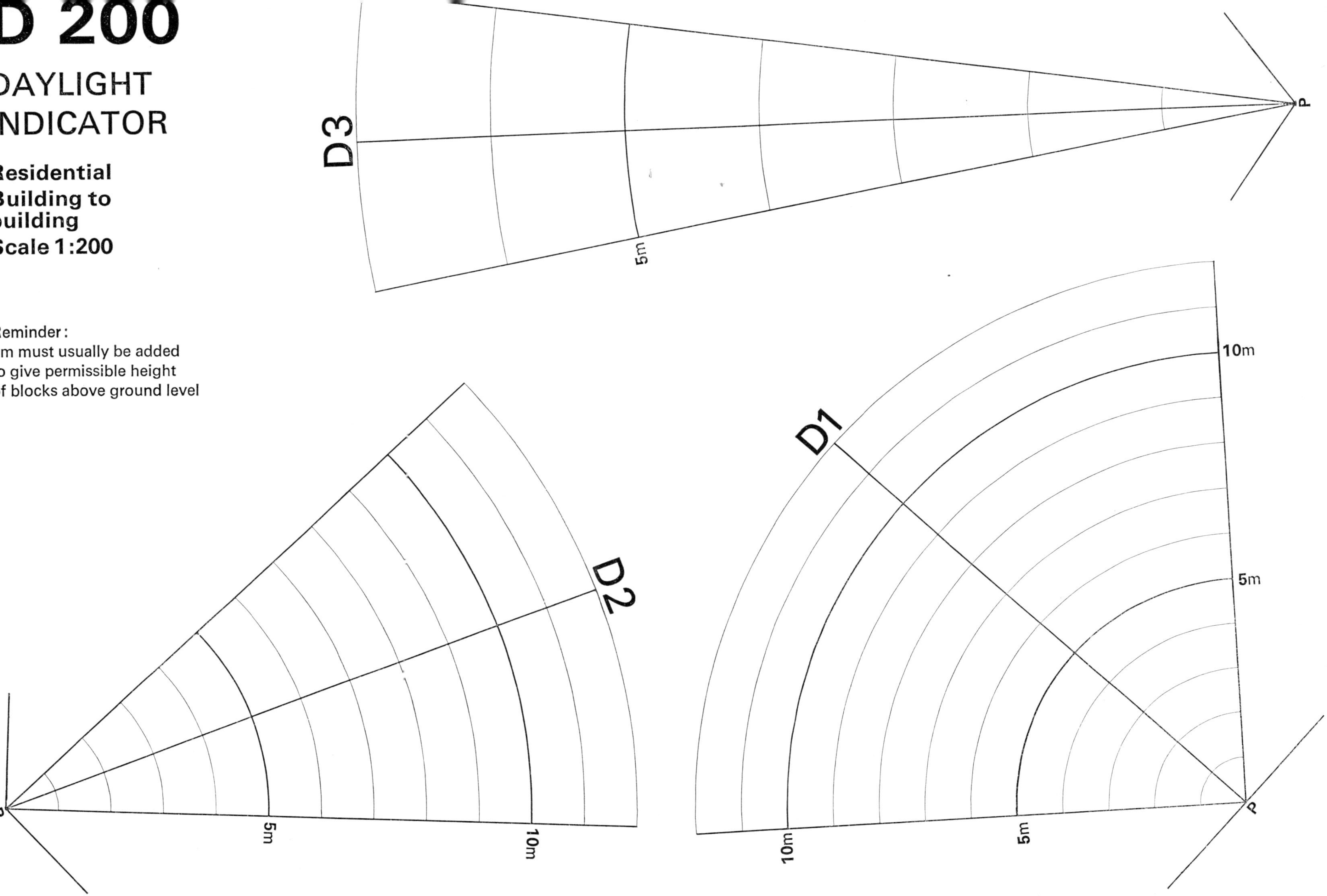

D1

10m

5m

5m

10m

P

D2

10m

5m

P

D3

5m

P

7.26   The method of use of the D indicators is to select the appropriate indicator and place P on the plan at the point to be tested on the side of a building, normally at 2 metres above ground level. D2 and D3 may be swivelled about P between positions in which the outer angle arms coincide with the building face. In D1 the outer angle arms form a straight line, which must coincide with the building face, and do not permit swivelling.

7.27   The block spacing criterion (3.6 and 3.14) is satisfied if, for any one indicator, the whole central angle is free of 'contravening obstructions'; contravening obstructions being those which are not entirely beyond the arc corresponding to their height relative to P. In the case of D2 and D3, if an indicator is partly satisfied in one angular position and partly in another, the horizontal angles satisfied may be added together. It is also admissible to add the extent of satisfaction of one indicator, expressed as a fraction of the central angle, to that of another of the set, provided there is no over-lapping.

7.28   The B indicators can be used and combined in the same way but are applied from the plot boundary (2 metres above ground level) inwards over the proposal site. Figures 24 to 27 illustrate the use of D and B indicators to test whether proposals for housing layouts satisfy the block spacing criteria for daylight.

7.29   To test AB of block ABCD (figure 24) where block EFGHJK is the only obstruction to light: apply indicator D3 turned to the left so that the outer angle arm on the indicator coincides with the side AB. Whatever the height of the obstruction, the section AL of side AB will have enough light 'round the side' to satisfy the daylight criterion (3.6). The section BM can be cleared in the same way. When using the D indicators one must take into consideration existing buildings beyond the boundaries of the proposal. In this case such buildings might have affected D3 by obstructing 'light round the side' of buildings in the layout.

7.30   To test the remaining section LM (figure 25): apply indicator D1 to the mid point between L and M, the outer angle arms of the indicator coinciding with the side of the building. A 13 metre arc drawn between the 10 and 15 metre arcs would nearly touch KJ. 13 metres is therefore about the 'permissible height' of the side KJ above the reference point. If the site is flat, add 2 metres for the 'permissible height' above ground, giving 15 metres. Note: the face KJ which faces south-west should be tested by the sunlight indicator.

7.31   In figure 26 blocks of housing form a 3-sided court. The D2 indicator is designed for this sort of case. To test side PQ apply the indicator D2 to the point on the face having the least open aspect namely P. The right-hand outer arm of the indicator should be laid along PQ. The inter-section of the northerly wing of the building with the arcs of the indicator show the 'permissible height' above the reference point to be about 11 metres. If the site is flat the 'permissible height' above ground is therefore 13 metres. The side PR facing north-east should be tested by the D2 or the D3 indicator. The south-east facing side RS should be tested by the sun-light indicator.

7.32   In figure 27 indicators are used to test whether or not the criterion (3.10) which protects the *residential* development potential of an adjoining plot is satisfied. To the boundary between the proposal and the adjoining plot apply indicator B3 to identify the sections up to L and M for which enough light is received 'round the side,' and then test the mid point be-tween L and M with the B1 indicator. The point of application is again 2 metres above ground level. In using the B indicators obstructions beyond the boundary of the proposal site should be ignored.

7.33   The C and A indicators are used respectively in the same way as the D and B indicators. The C indicators are applied to the sides of proposed

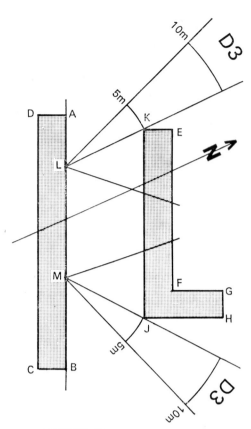

FIGURE 24

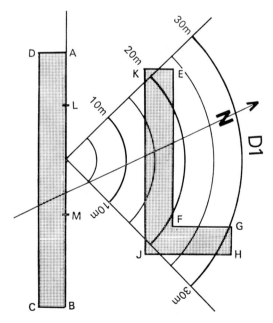

FIGURE 25

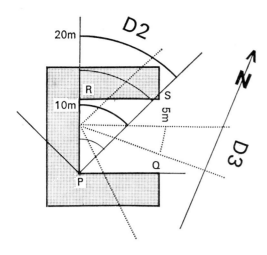

FIGURE 26

buildings to test non-residential building proposals; the A indicators are applied to the boundary of the proposal site to protect the non-residential development potential of adjoining plots. One should use these indicators with discretion, taking account of the particular non-residential use in question (3.7).

7.34   The examples above illustrate that, for a block spacing check on level ground, one must add two metres to the heights given by the arcs to get 'permissible heights' *above ground level*. This is the one important change from the previous procedure: the 1964 indicators give the 'permissible height' above ground level directly.

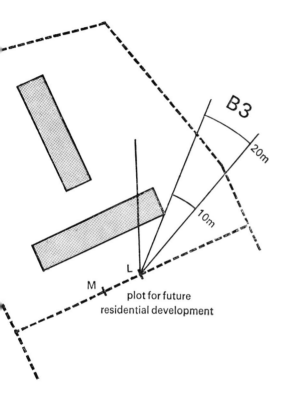

FIGURE 27

Considerations for design

8

8.1   This study is mainly concerned with the spacing of blocks to provide good sunlight and daylight in the local environment considered broadly (AIM 1, 2.3). Its purpose is not to give comprehensive guidance about achieving good conditions in detail (AIM 2). However, as has been shown, planning and architecture interpenetrate. Good planning may be frustrated by bad architectural design. For instance blocks of dwellings, properly spaced, may have play spaces in permanent shadow and inadequate windows overhung by balconies. Sources of guidance for architects have been mentioned, notably the British Standards Institution's code for daylight (Appendix C), but it may be helpful here to draw the attention of architects to a number of design points, particularly in regard to sunlight which, at the present time (1971), is not covered by an up-to-date code of practice. This chapter may also help planning authorities in the occasional difficult case that needs to be considered in some detail.

8.2   A good design not merely avoids deprivation of sunlight and daylight but provides conditions for the maximum sunlight and daylight that can reasonably be achieved. Most of the layout will have much more than minimum requirements.

8.3   Aiming at optimum as opposed to minimum conditions, one may need to take special account of penetrating, as opposed to glancing, sunlight, of sunlight available at times when working people are at home and of sunlight in winter and summer as well as early spring. One should also consider how roads, paths and spaces of various kinds, with their various sunlight requirements, can best be fitted into the gaps required to ensure good block placing, privacy from overlooking and pleasant views. Various aspects of housing layout design and their inter-relations are considered in a series of bulletins and papers being published by the Department of the Environment.

8.4   In their own development work local authorities will need to ensure that their different departments collaborate in designing for sunlight and daylight as in other spheres. In particular the skill necessary to make measurements relating to sunlight and daylight should be available as a common service to local authority architects and planners.

8.5   The measurements on which the following paragraphs are based were made by the Sunscan (Appendix A).

Open ground and sunlight

8.6   Sunlight is required not only inside buildings but also in gardens and sitting-out places, in play spaces, shopping precincts and on footpaths. Sun is probably not less valued in the open than inside the house; and, because people go outside more often in spring, summer and autumn than in winter, plenty of sun on the ground in the months between April and October is just as much to be aimed at as a little in winter.

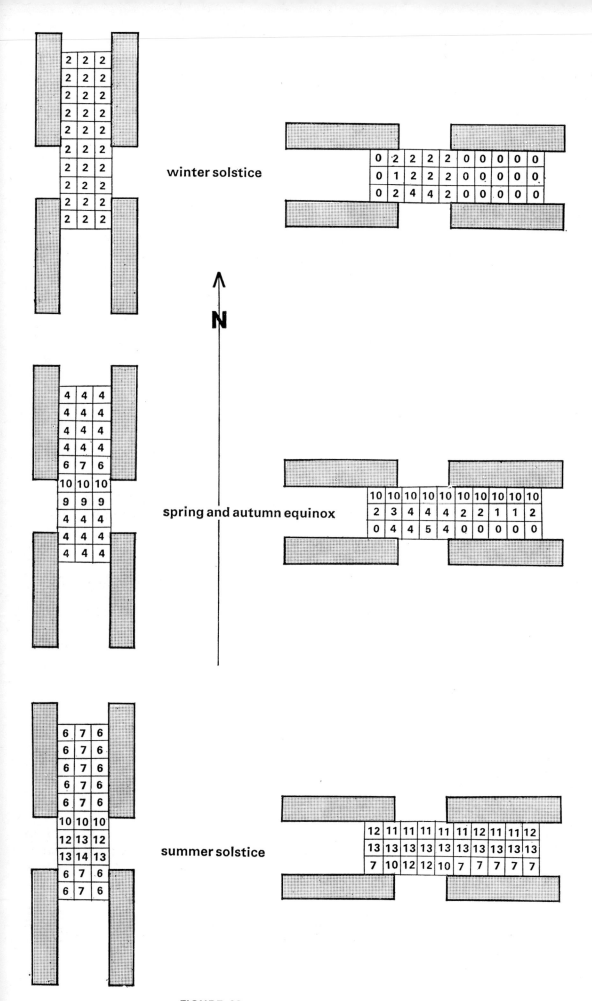

winter solstice

0	2	2	2	2	0	0	0	0	0
0	1	2	2	2	0	0	0	0	0
0	2	4	4	2	0	0	0	0	0

N

spring and autumn equinox

10	10	10	10	10	10	10	10	10	10
2	3	4	4	4	2	2	1	1	2
0	4	4	5	4	0	0	0	0	0

summer solstice

12	11	11	11	11	11	12	11	11	12
13	13	13	13	13	13	13	13	13	13
7	10	12	12	10	7	7	7	7	7

FIGURE 28
53°N. Height of blocks h. Spacing of blocks 2h. Figures show duration of sunlight in hours at the positions indicated. These layouts easily satisfy the residential block spacing criteria (3.5, 3.6).

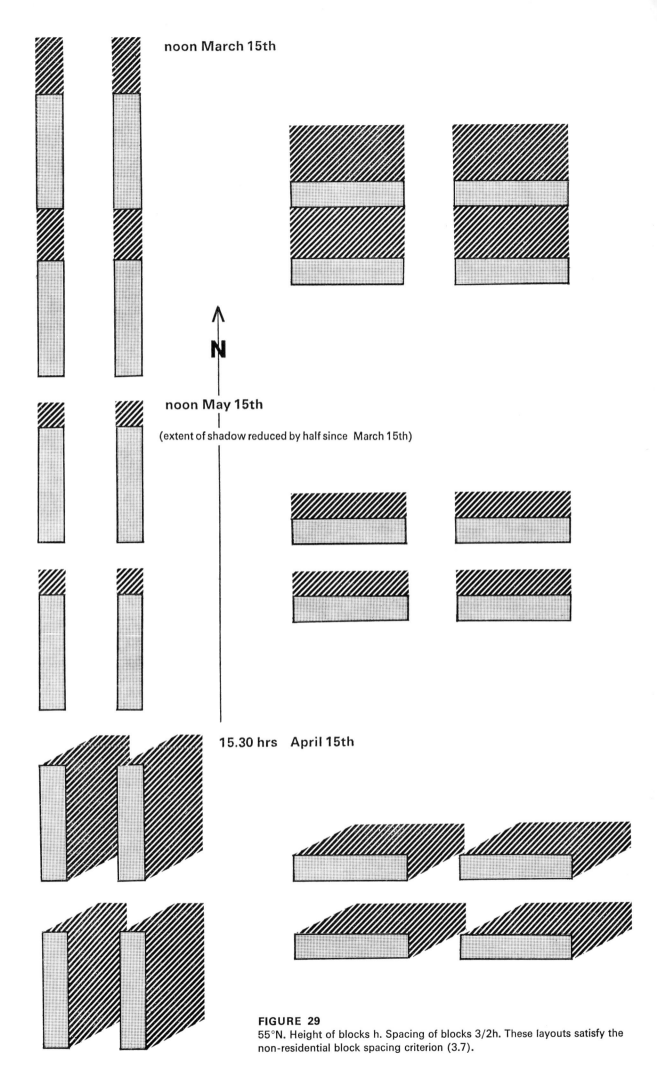

noon March 15th

N

noon May 15th

(extent of shadow reduced by half since March 15th)

15.30 hrs   April 15th

FIGURE 29
55°N. Height of blocks h. Spacing of blocks 3/2h. These layouts satisfy the
non-residential block spacing criterion (3.7).

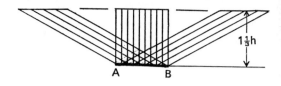

height of A B and C D = h

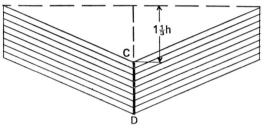

FIGURE 30
At equinox the shadow of a point at height h moves in a straight line on the horizontal datum plane at about $1\frac{1}{3}$h distant from the vertical. The building face AB produces a shadow which remains the same in area all day long. That of CD varies in area from infinite to nil to infinite.

8.7   Figure 28 illustrates the radical difference between seasonal patterns of the duration of potential sunlight on the ground in differently oriented layouts. The overall total for the 4 seasons together is much the same in the 2 layouts; but in mid-winter all the ground in the first layout (in which the blocks have sides facing east and west) has 2 hours of potential sunlight per day, whereas in the second most of this ground gets no sunlight at all. In spring the distribution between blocks is even in the first layout but very uneven in the second; only in midsummer does nearly all the ground in the second layout receive sun for long periods.

8.8.   Figure 29 illustrates another big difference, namely in the time of day at which sunlight and shadow occur. Between blocks in the first layout in this figure maximum sunlight is received at midday; in the second it is received in the early morning and late afternoon. In summer the noon shadow is very small in the first layout but always considerable in the second. On April 15 the shadow in the first would extend right across the space between the blocks at 8.30 hours, rapidly diminishing in size until noon, when none of the space between the main faces would be in shadow, and then rapidly increasing to extend across the space again at 15.30 hours. In the second layout the shadows cover rather more than half the space between the blocks at noon but leave rather more than half in sunlight in morning and afternoon.

8.9   Certain obvious conclusions may be drawn: the shadowed area to the north of long blocks with sides facing north and south is generally more suitable for, say, car parking than for recreation; on the other hand, in accessible places between blocks with sides facing east and west, the lunch-hour sunshine is appreciated by city workers. But sunlight regimes are complex: the pattern of potential sunlight on the ground changes from month to month and from hour to hour, as well as between one disposition of buildings and another; to design for sunlight on the ground one must decide at what hours and at what season it is needed.

8.10   Figure 31 shows that noon shadows lengthen and then diminish very rapidly from month to month through the winter: they are some seven times longer in mid-winter than in mid-summer. For a month or two in winter a low wall or hedge running east and west could overshadow the whole of a relatively narrow garden: a series of such narrow gardens would then catch the sunlight only on the south facing walls. The two-hour pattern shown in figure 28 (winter solstice) can only be achieved if there are no such obstructions.

8.11   The times of day referred to throughout this study are Local Apparent Time (LAT) or sun time. One hour, more or less, must be added to give British summer time. (See Appendix B for more details on this subject.)

Buildings and sunlight

8.12   The problem of getting sun *into buildings* is quite different. The aspect of façades is the most important consideration here. *Spacing* of buildings may not affect sunlight of upper storeys but *aspect* affects it at all levels. A northerly aspect, even if there are no obstructions to the view, can have no sun for half the year and little in summer.

8.13   The following table shows potential sunlight of over 10° altitude available to windows with different aspects at the winter and summer solstices and the spring and autumn equinoxes. The table applies specifically at 53° north latitude but, approximately, over the whole country. Above 10° altitude the view is assumed to be clear of obstructions.

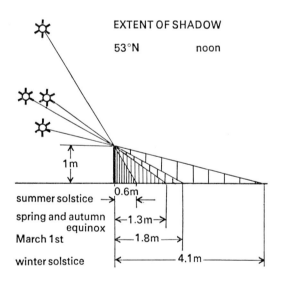

EXTENT OF SHADOW

53°N   noon

1m

summer solstice →   0.6m ←
spring and autumn equinox ←1.3m→
March 1st   ←——1.8m——→
winter solstice   ←————4.1m————→

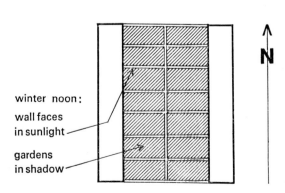

winter noon:
wall faces
in sunlight
gardens
in shadow

N

FIGURE 31

aspect	season	total duration (hours)	time of day available	duration of penetrating sun (over 45° to plane of window)
N	winter	nil	nil	nil
	spring and autumn	nil	nil	nil
	summer	5	early morning, evening	nil
NE	winter	nil	nil	nil
	spring and autumn	2	early morning	nil
	summer	5	early and mid morning	2
E	winter	2	all morning	nil
	spring and autumn	5	all morning	2
	summer	7	all morning	5
SE	winter	4	all day	2
	spring and autumn	7	all day until mid afternoon	5
	summer	9	all day until mid afternoon	2
S	winter	4	all day	4
	spring and autumn	10	all day	5
	summer	10	all day	0
SW	winter	4	all day	2
	spring and autumn	7	all day from mid morning	5
	summer	9	all day from mid morning	2
W	winter	2	all afternoon	nil
	spring and autumn	5	all afternoon	2
	summer	7	all afternoon	5
NW	winter	nil	nil	nil
	spring and autumn	2	from mid afternoon	nil
	summer	5	afternoon and evening	2

Note: The dates taken to represent the seasons in the second column are those of the solstices and equinoxes.

8.14 One should not necessarily conclude that the *orientation of the building block* is always crucial. If dwellings have two opposite aspects, front and back, one at least should provide sunshine in rooms; consequently the *disposition of rooms and windows inside the building* to take advantage of sunshine will be more important. But if freedom of internal design is limited, as in single aspect dwellings, the only way to get sun, even in upper storeys, may be by correct orientation of the block. Single aspect flats on each side of a block must share the potential sunlight: if one side has more than half the other will have correspondingly less than half; and of the total sunshine that has to be shared some 3 hours will be glancing sunshine that hardly penetrates the windows. In this case the constraints on spacing are also severe; if shadow from another building falls on single aspect flats the chances are it will reduce sunshine unacceptably (figure 12).

8.15   A layout composed of long parallel blocks, oriented so that the sides of the blocks face east and west, has the advantage that rooms on both sides of the block may get sunlight some time in the middle of the day throughout the year. It has the disadvantage that the blocks must be relatively low or widely spaced if the duration of sunlight is not to be short. Moreover much of the sunlight is glancing sunlight that lights the ground but does not penetrate windows (figure 32).

8.16   In the same layout, oriented so that the sides of the blocks face north and south, living rooms (facing south) may get long lasting, penetrating sunlight for most of the year, but not get any sun at all in winter, for a number of months that depends on the height and spacing of the blocks. Very little useful sunlight falls on windows on the north sides of the blocks.

8.17   The advantages of these 2 orientations, in which windows face towards the cardinal points, are to some degree combined in intermediate orientations: sunlight reaches south-easterly or south-westerly facing windows in winter, lasts for a long time each day in summer, spring and autumn, and penetrates into rooms. Some useful sunlight also falls on the other side of the blocks. In these intermediate orientations the sunlight criterion, three hours of potential sunlight on March 1 (3.5), is satisfied by blocks that can be closer or higher, and consequently at higher density, than those in either of the 'cardinal point' orientations.

8.18   The illustrations (figure 32) assume a latitude of 53° north. The following table shows for 3 latitudes the date on which, from a south-

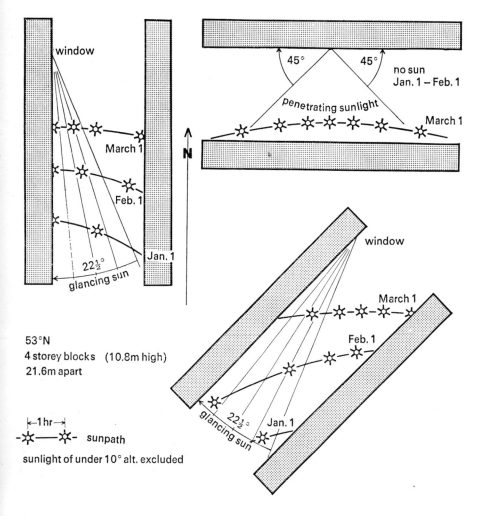

53°N
4 storey blocks   (10.8m high)
21.6m apart

|←1 hr→|
-✱——✱- sunpath

sunlight of under 10° alt. excluded

FIGURE 32

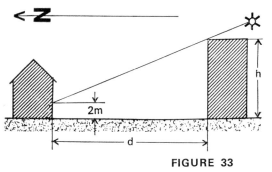

FIGURE 33

facing window, the sun is first visible over the top of a long building opposite (figure 33). The height (h) of the obstructing building is taken as 10 metres and its distance is varied.

Distance away of 10 m high obstruction	Date on which sun is first visible		
	51°N Latitude	53°N Latitude	55°N Latitude
10 m	20 March	25 March	30 March
15 m	20 February	26 February	3 March
20 m	1 February	7 February	14 February
25 m	14 January	24 January	1 February
30 m	visible all the year	9 January	20 January

8.19   As has been said, a common defect in layout design is the juxtaposition of blocks at right angles so that the one towards the south casts a shadow on the one towards the north (figure 16). Any 'opposed' layout, i.e. one in which some blocks are parallel and others are at right angles to them, unless it is carefully designed with adequate gaps for sunlight, is likely to produce juxtapositions of this kind, cutting off sun from windows and from the ground, especially if the sides of blocks face towards the cardinal points, east, west, north and south. Opposed layouts with intermediate orientations, with blocks facing between cardinal points, are not so seriously affected: they may be designed at high densities to provide good sunlight regimes (figure 15).

8.20   Figure 34 illustrates the effect on the parallel layout shown in figure 28 of inserting, at right angles, short blocks of the same height. In the places indicated ground-floor windows do not now get 3 hours of sunlight on March 1. Moreover sunlight on the ground is reduced (compare figures 28 and 34), and the view from windows will contain more shadows on the ground and on buildings.

Windows, daylight and view

8.21   In planning for sunlight the proper disposition of buildings is a necessary condition of success: if a building face is in shadow no opening in it can admit any sunlight. The same is not true of daylight: the handicap of a poor disposition of buildings can, in theory at least, be overcome by having large enough windows. This chapter has accordingly considered layout in terms of sunlight. It remains to consider window and room arrangements, and then balconies and projections, largely in terms of the daylight admitted by the window and the view seen through it. This treatment is not comprehensive. The sunlight regime inside rooms is affected not only by the disposition of buildings but also by window and room design, a subject which the British Standards Institution intend to deal with in the new code of practice for sunlight in course of preparation (1971). Nothing is said here about the function of rooms: again the existing and proposed codes of practice of the British Standards Institution will provide guidance.

8.22   The sky is normally brighter at the zenith than at the horizon, and the flux of low altitude daylight is often blocked by buildings and vegetation. If windows were not required to admit sunlight, which for most of the year has a maximum altitude of less than 40°, or a view of the ground as well as the sky, their remaining daylight function might better be served by horizontal or inclined skylights. *The normal multi-purpose vertical window, if it is to admit daylight reasonably efficiently, needs to have a high window head.*

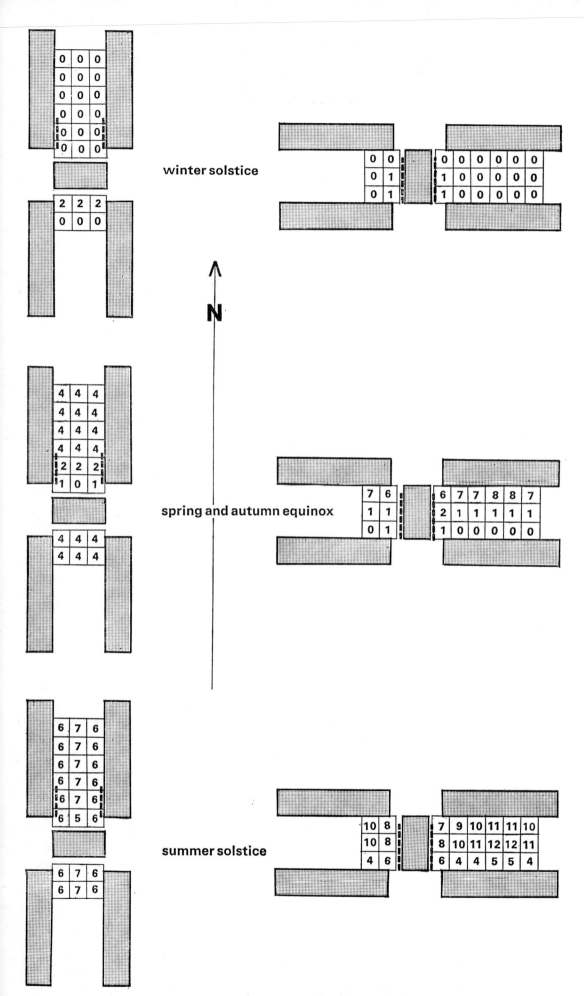

FIGURE 34
53°N. Height of blocks h. Spacing of blocks 2h. Figures show duration of sunlight in hours at the positions indicated. Broken lines show where the sunlight criterion is not satisfied.

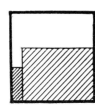

Cill level view through a window 1.1m square taken from the reference point.

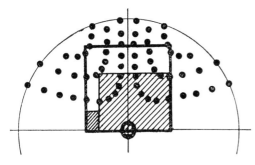

The Sky Component given by the number of dots in the visible sky (13) is 1.3%.

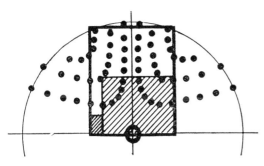

Raising the window head by 300mm increases the Sky Component to 2.6%.

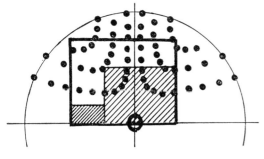

Increasing the width of the window by 300mm increases the Sky Component from 1.3% to 1.9% at the same reference point. In this case however, the widening brings into view a gap in buildings which accounts for about half the extra Sky Component and also improves the view.

FIGURE 35
1:50 scale
The reference point is 1.5m inside the room from the window at cill level. Measurements are taken by applying the Environmental Advisory Service overlay 3.1 giving Sky Component of C I E standard overcast sky; glass transmission 0.85.

8.23 This is particularly important if there is a high façade opposite. A combination of a high opposing façade and a low window head will tend to cut out light from the back part of the room and make it impossible to see the sky except from near the window; the deeper the room the worse the effect will be. Increasing the width of the window will not solve the problem.

8.24 A *wide* window is however particularly useful in two situations. First if the outside obstruction only extends part way across the view, i.e. if there is light 'round the side', a window which extends laterally to allow this gap to be seen will improve both the lighting and the view. Second, if the room is wide and not deep, a wide window, though it may not admit as much light as a high window, will distribute it more effectively.

8.25 In short, the optimum shape of the window is related to the form of the obstruction outside and the shape of the room. A high window is usually needed to give adequate light and, particularly, to light a deep room where there is a high continuous external obstruction. A wide window is needed to light a wide room and to take advantage of a gap at the side of an external obstruction.

8.26 As regards view: a high window head is usually necessary to include sky and cloudscape within it. Again a wide window may be needed where it can bring into the view gaps in the opposing buildings, but not where, for instance, it exposes a blank wall usually in shadow.

8.27 Another important feature of view is the way the scene is lit, particularly by sunlight; this depends largely on the aspect of the window. Usually views to east or west are more sunlit than views to north or south, views to south being the least sunlit. In views to east or west the pattern of shadow and sunlight on buildings and ground changes from hour to hour providing a variety of lighting. In north- and south-facing views shadow moves more slowly; a feature that is sunlit or in shadow in the morning may still be so in the afternoon.

Projections and balconies

8.28 Projections and balconies visible through windows may be regarded as screens drawn part way over the opening, projections being drawn across from the side and balconies down from the top. To think of them in this way enables a designer to apply general notions of window design (8.21 to 8.27) to the effective unscreened part of the window, bearing in mind that the 'effective window' will vary in shape according to the position of the observer: the screening effect will be less from the back than from the front of the room (figure 36).

8.29 Even a relatively low projection seen through a window, a single-storey garage or kitchen at ground level, tends to reduce the width of the opening, though some sky may be visible above it from some viewpoints. It will always reduce and change the distribution of daylight in the room but whether the effect on daylight or the view is serious depends on whether the projection hides what would otherwise be a useful gap in the external obstructions.

8.30 The effect on sunlight may often be serious. If the projection is on the southerly side of the window it produces, in miniature, exactly the kind of juxtaposition of perpendicular blocks that should be avoided (5.5). If it is on the northerly side it may obstruct a sunlit view. Projections tend to be in shadow for long periods since they may stand either in their own shadow or in the shadow of the main building (figure 37).

8.31   A projection may, of course, be formed by the recessing of one dwelling in relation to another in the same terrace.

8.32   A balcony visible through a window, by reducing the effective head height of the window, reduces the amount of sky in the view and the amount of what is likely to be the brightest and least obstructed daylight entering the window. The loss will be proportionately greatest if the sky is already partially obscured by a continuous façade opposite (figure 38). The effect on sunlight may be to cut off any high altitude summer sunlight that would otherwise be available in the middle of the day, but not to obstruct any available winter sunlight, since this comes in at a low altitude.

8.33   Clearly the effect of balconies and projections must be considered in relation to external obstructions. In parts of a layout in which block spacing only just satisfies the sunlight and daylight criteria any balconies and projections visible from well inside living rooms or kitchens are likely to reduce sunlight and daylight to below acceptable minima. Their effect on the daylight, sunlight and view of windows near them should not be under estimated.

FIGURE 36

FIGURE 37
View through an east-facing window at 15.00 hrs, March 1, latitude 53°N, in an open layout of 2/3 storey housing. A single storey kitchen or garage projection, though on the north side of the window, stands in the shadow of the main building and obscures part of a sunlit gap in the layout.

FIGURE 38

Other methods of measurement

Sunscan

A.1   This is a small portable instrument which came into production in 1971. It is used on *plans* of buildings and layouts at a variety of scales to provide information about sunlight, shadow, daylight and solar heating. It operates by producing a fine ray of light to simulate a ray either from the sun or, if daylight is being studied, from a small patch of sky. The ray strikes the plan in a speck of light. In particular the Sunscan can be used to measure accurately and quickly, at any point in the layout, the Sky Component available between given angular limits and the hours of potential sunlight available in a given month. It thus can check whether the block spacing criteria are satisfied and provide information that may be needed in cases to which the criteria do not apply as for instance in the safeguarding of existing buildings. The Sunscan can also be used in the design process (chapter 8), or in research, to determine how any one variable affects a situation when the others are held constant; thus the potential availability of the sun can be related to any one of its determinants, latitude, season, time of day, height and distance of obstruction. Within a room the Sky Factor, Sky Component and Externally Reflected Component can be similarly related to window head height, window width and the height and distance of external obstructions. (Manufacturers: Research Engineers Ltd, Orsman Road, Shoreditch N1.)

Supplementary sunlight and daylight indicators

A.2   Details necessary for the construction of sunlight indicators for February 21 and November 22, for latitudes 51° 30', 52° 30' 53° 30' and 55° north, were given in Planning Bulletin 5, Planning for Daylight and Sunlight (1964), Table 1 on page 20. Similarly details necessary for the construction of sunlight indicators covering 9, 8, 7 and 6 months of the year for latitude 51° 30' were given in Tables 3 and 4 of that publication.

A.3   In place of the tables referred to, the following formulae can be used for the construction of sunlight indicators for any latitude and season:
i the formula for solar altitude (a):

$$\sin a = \cos \theta \ \cos \delta \ \cos t + \sin \theta \ \sin \delta$$

where δ = solar declination
t = hours angle from noon (15° = 1 hour)
θ = latitude,
ii the formula giving the solar azimuth angle (A) for the construction of the hour lines:

$$\sin A = \sin t \ \frac{\cos \delta}{\cos a}$$

The value of δ (declination) for the dates in the tables mentioned above are approximately as follows:

6 February/6 November	−15° 48'
21 February/22 October	−10° 48'
7 March/8 October	−5° 35'
21 March/23 September (equinox)	0°.

The value of δ for 1 March, the date specified in the criterion (3.5), should be taken as −7° 45'.

A4.   It is possible also to construct daylight indicators supplementary to the indicators numbered 1, 2 and 3 in each of the sets A B C and D. For any central angle chosen, a 'window' is defined, horizontally, by this angle and, vertically, by the angle of maximum elevation specified in the appropriate block spacing criterion (3.6, 3.7, 3.10 or 3.11) and, on the lower side, by the vertical angle subtended by the arcs of 'permissible height' to be drawn in the indicator. This 'window' should give a Sky Component, on the horizontal plane at the vertex of the indicator, of the amount specified in the appropriate criterion.

Waldram diagram

A.5   The Waldram diagram is used for determining the Sky Component at a point in a room. It consists of a grid of lines, some straight and some curved, in relation to which the outlines of window openings and external obstructions can be plotted. A systematically deformed picture results in which the Sky Component is found directly by measurement of the area of the space between window openings and external obstructions.

A.6   The great advantage of the Waldram diagram is that it can be used reliably for the most complicated forms of obstruction, but it involves making a number of angular measurements or calculations, both on the layout plan and on cross sections. Its use is fully described in the British Standard Code of Practice CP3: chapter I: part 1 (1964.)

Building Research Station daylight protractors

A7.   The daylight protractors issued by the Building Research Station are for the determination, from plans and vertical sections, of the Sky Component and Externally Reflected Component for any point in a room. The protractors, applied first to a vertical section of the room under examination, give a direct reading of what the Sky Component would be if the window were infinitely long. An auxiliary protractor is then applied on a plan of the same room to allow the appropriate correction to be made for the actual length of the window. Various versions of the protractors are produced to apply to various kinds of window openings, vertical, horizontal, sloping, glazed and unglazed.

A.8   The daylight protractors are available from
Her Majesty's Stationery Office, price 25p each,
and full instructions for their use are contained in *BRS Daylight Protractors* by J. Longmore. Her Majesty's Stationery Office, 1968, price $52\frac{1}{2}$p.

Environmental Advisory Service charts and overlays

A.9   These charts and overlays embody the technique described in the book *Windows and Environment* published in 1969 on behalf of the Environmental Advisory Service, Pilkington Brothers Limited, St Helens.

A.10   The daylight overlays are placed on an ordinary perspective view as seen through the window. The Sky Component and Externally Reflected Component are estimated by the counting of dots in the unobstructed part of the sky.

A.11   The sun position overlay is also used with the ordinary perspective view through the window. A correct selection of the overlay, and correct setting and orientation on the elevation of the window, give the sunpaths at various dates of the year.

Calculation of the Internally Reflected Component (IRC)

A.12   In regard to daylight, methods listed above provide measures of Sky Component and Externally Reflected Component (ERC) but not of the Internally Reflected Component (IRC). An accepted method of estimating the Internally Reflected Component is given in the British Standard Code of Practice CP3: chapter I: part 1 (1964). The calculation of this component of daylight is normally part of the process of calculating the total Daylight Factor.

A.13   The calculation may be based on the Building Research Station table which gives the minimum and average value of this component for a room of normal size assuming an external angle of obstruction of 20°. One needs to know the proportion of the window area to the floor area and the average reflection factors of the floor, ceiling and walls. Alternatively a nomogram can be used or, if greater precision is needed, the Building Research Station inter-reflection formula. Information on these methods is given in the Code of Practice mentioned above and in the Building Research Station's Digest 42. A different method of calculating the IRC is given in 'Windows and Environment' (A.9).

Calculation of solar heat gain

A.14   The amount of solar radiation transmitted into a room can be calculated from the size of the window, the elevation of the sun, the angle between the sun ray and the normal to the window, etc. This subject is dealt with in Current Papers 37, 39 and supplement to 39, of the Building Research Station.

Sunshine and shadow studied on models

A.15   The sunshine and shadow in a layout may be simulated on a scale model placed under a source of parallel or nearly parallel rays of light (such as a distant electric bulb) at an angle corresponding to that of the sun at the time of day, season, and latitude to be considered. This angle can be obtained by the Sunscan (A.1) or by one of the methods described in 'Windows and Environment' of the Environmental Advisory Service (A.9).

A.16   The shadow can be adjusted by movement of the light source relative to the model, or by the appropriate tilting and orientation of the model under a fixed light source. The Heliodon, devised in the early 1930s at the Building Research Station, and the Shelliodon devised at the Scottish Development Department, employ the method of tilting and orientating the model, the adjustments governing the relative position of the light and the model being calibrated to give the latitude, season and time of day.

Artificial skies

A.17   A technique for assessing Daylight Factor under a luminous surface simulating the sky is used at the Building Research Station and some other centres. Scale model rooms with window openings, and surfaces correctly coloured, are placed under the artificial sky and measurements made by photo-cells in appropriate positions in the rooms. In large-scale models, arranged so that the designer can put his head up through a hole in the floor, conditions can be assessed by direct observation.

A.18   This method has the advantage that not only the Sky Component and the Externally Reflected Component but also the Internally Reflected Component can be directly simulated.

TNO Meter *(Instituut vor Gezondheidstechniek TNO Holland)*

A.19 Measurements relating to sunlight and daylight in *existing* as opposed to proposed buildings can be effectively carried out by this Dutch instrument which consists of a lens convex on the upper surface and flat on the lower surface. On the flat underside can be attached sunpath diagrams or dot diagrams of Sky Component. The instrument is taken to the reference point, in the room which is being studied, and held horizontally. The window frame, the external obstruction and the unobscured sky are reflected in the convex surface. From the length of sunpaths, or the number of dots, in the unobscured sky, the potential duration of sunlight at different seasons, and the Sky Component, can be assessed.

A.20 An alternative method of assessing conditions in existing buildings is to make a photographic record of windows from appropriate reference points and subsequently analyse this with the aid of plans and overlays.

Definitions

Daylight Factor

B.1   A measure of the daylight illumination on a given plane at a point, relative to that prevailing simultaneously out of doors. It is the ratio of the daylight illumination at a point on a given plane due to the light received directly or indirectly from a sky of assumed or known luminance distribution, to the illumination on a horizontal plane due to an unobstructed hemisphere of this sky. Direct sunlight is excluded for both values of illumination.

B.2   The Daylight Factor comprises light received directly from the sky (Sky Component), light received directly by reflection from external surfaces (Externally Reflected Component) and by reflection and inter-reflection from internal surfaces (Internally Reflected Component).

Sky Component

B.3.   That component of the Daylight Factor received directly from the sky. It is the ratio of that part of the daylight illumination at a point on a given plane which is received directly from a sky of assumed or known luminance distribution, to the illumination on a horizontal plane due to an unobstructed hemisphere of this sky. Direct sunlight is excluded for both values of illumination.

Externally Reflected Component

B.4   That component of the Daylight Factor received directly by reflection from external surfaces. It is the ratio of that part of the daylight illumination at a point on a given plane which is received directly from externally reflecting surfaces illuminated directly or indirectly by a sky of assumed or known luminance distribution, to the illumination on a horizontal plane due to an unobstructed hemisphere of this sky. Contributions of direct sunlight to the luminances of externally reflecting surfaces and to the illumination of the comparison plane are excluded.

Internally Reflected Component

B.5   That component of the Daylight Factor received by reflection and inter-reflection from internal surfaces. It is the ratio of that part of the daylight illumination at a point on a given plane which is received from internally reflecting surfaces, the sky being of assumed or known luminance distribution, to the illumination on a horizontal plane due to an unobstructed hemisphere of this sky. Contributions of direct sunlight to the luminance of internally reflecting surfaces and to the illumination of the comparison plane are excluded.

CIE Standard Overcast Sky

B.6   A completely overcast sky for which the ratio of its luminance at an altitude θ above the horizon to the luminance at the zenith is assumed to be

$$\frac{1 + 2 \sin \theta}{3}$$

Note. In this study the CIE Standard Overcast Sky is assumed for daylight calculations.

Sky Factor

B.7   For unglazed openings the Sky Factor is identical with the Sky Component of a sky of uniform luminance (as opposed to the CIE sky which has a greater luminance at the zenith than at the horizon).

Working plane

B.8   The working plane is the plane on which measurements and calculations of daylight are made. Unless otherwise stated the plane is assumed to be horizontal.
Note. The plane to which the Sky Component refers in this study is a horizontal plane.

Horizontal angle of acceptance

B.9   The horizontal angles of acceptance illustrated in figures 1 to 3 are defined by the horizontal angular limits for the acceptance of daylight for the purposes of the block spacing criteria (3.6, 3.7, 3.10 and 3.11).

Vertical angle of acceptance

B.10   The vertical angles of acceptance illustrated in figures 1 to 3 are defined by the vertical angular limits for the acceptance of daylight for the purposes of the block spacing criteria (3.6, 3.7, 3.10 and 3.11).

10° line

B.11   The 10° lines marked on the sunlight indicators are lines showing the bearing at which the sun has an altitude of 10°.

Local Apparent Time or sun time

B.12   Throughout this study wherever time is referred to 'Local Apparent Time' or 'sun time' is meant. Local Apparent Time (LAT) is the time which would be given by a clock adjusted each day to read 12 noon when the sun is due south. To derive Greenwich Mean Time (GMT) from Local Apparent Time two adjustments have to be made to LAT.

B.13   The first adjustment takes account of the fact that the length of the solar day is not a constant 24 hours throughout the year. The accumulation of small differences results in sun time (LAT) running fast or slow relative to a steady 24 hours a day time known as Local Mean Time (LMT). The adjustment to equate LAT to LMT is known as the 'Equation of Time'; it has a minimum value of −14 minutes in February and a maximum of +16 minutes in November.

B.14   The second adjustment is to take account of longitude; this involves adding (for places west of the Greenwich Meridian) or subtracting (for places east) 4 minutes for each degree of longitude. When British summer time is in force it can be derived by adding one hour to GMT.

B.15   The table below gives approximately, for 8 big towns, the adjustments necessary to convert LAT's into GMT's at the date of the summer solstice.

Town	Longitude	June 21 Equation of Time (minutes)	Adjustment for longitude (minutes)	Total adjustment to convert LAT to GMT (minutes)
Birmingham	1° 55′ W	−2	+ 8	+ 6
Bristol	2° 35′ W	−2	+10	+ 8
Cardiff	3° 10′ W	−2	+13	+11
Leeds	1° 35′ W	−2	+ 6	+ 4
Liverpool	3° 00′ W	−2	+12	+10
London	0°	−2	0	− 2
Manchester	2° 15′ W	−2	+ 9	+ 7
Newcastle-upon-Tyne	1° 35′ W	−2	+ 6	+ 4

Other criteria

Sunlight criteria

C.1   The British Standard Code of Practice (1945) of the British Standards Institution is at present (1971) being revised. This 1945 code was one basis for Planning Bulletin 5 (1964). Its recommendations were:

'a. in living rooms and, where practicable, in kitchens and bedrooms also, one of the windows forming the main source of daylight should be so placed that sunlight can enter for at least one hour at some time of the day, during not less than the 10 months of the year from February to November. It is preferable for sunlight to enter living rooms in the afternoon and kitchens and bedrooms in the morning.

b. In teaching rooms the principal windows should be so placed that sunlight can enter for about 2 hours in the morning throughout the year.

c. Larders should be sited so that they are protected from the heat of the sun.
Note. Sunlight should not be considered to enter a room if the horizontal angle between the sun's rays and the plane of the window is less than $22\frac{1}{2}°$.'

C.2   It was also recommended as follows:
'In making provision for adequate sunlight in winter, excessive insolation in summer may result, particularly in teaching rooms in schools, and may call for the provision of means, either fixed or adjustable, for the exclusion of the sun's rays. This contingency should receive due consideration at the planning stage.
The area of ground in permanent shadow around houses, flats and school buildings should be reasonably small, and it is desirable that the sun should have as much access as possible to all façades of the building. This will depend on the shape of the building and its orientation. With a long building the worst condition will obtain when the major axis lies east and west. The best condition will obtain when the major axis lies either north-east and south-west or south-east and north-west. The major axis lying north and south will generally produce small shadowed areas.'
(British Standard Code of Practice CP5: 1945. Re-numbered CP3 chapter I(B) Sunlight. Houses, Flats and Schools only.)

C.3.   The British Standards Institution's code drafting committee on sunlight is at present engaged in a more complete investigation with a view to producing a revised code of practice. This study takes account of the work done by the British Standards Institution's committee so far.

C4.   The Scottish Housing Handbook. 1. Housing Layout (revised edition 1958) discusses the problems of sunlight in layout.

Daylight criteria

C.5   The British Standard Code of Practice. CP3: chapter I: part 1 (1964) of the British Standards Institution makes the following recommendations about amounts of daylight that should be provided as minima for good practice in dwellings.

'a. *Kitchens*. In domestic kitchens the tasks which are most demanding visually are centred on fixed points such as the cooker, sink and preparation table. It is recommended, therefore, that a daylight factor of 2% be provided over 50% of the total floor area within a minimum of 50 sq ft, and with the cooker, sink and preparation table sited well within these zones. The sink is usually placed underneath the window but, if for planning reasons, it is desired to place the sink in any other position, particular care is required to avoid the housewife being obliged to stand in her own light. Where the working surface is placed directly under the window the sill should not be more than 6 ins above it.

For the purpose of implementing this standard at the design stage, it is recommended that the following reflection factors be assumed for the main surfaces of one room. They include some allowance for furniture and deterioration of decorations and should be considered the maximum reflection factors practicable:

      walls   = 40% reflection factor (approximate Munsell value 7)
      floor   = 15% reflection factor (approximate Munsell value 4.5)
      ceiling = 70% reflection factor (approximate Munsell value 9).

b. *Living rooms*. A minimum daylight factor of 1% should cover at least 75 sq ft, and the penetration of the 1% zone should extend at least half the depth of the room facing the main window. For rooms of unusual shape, or where the main window is sited at one end of the room, the provision of light from windows in more than one wall assists a satisfactory distribution of daylight, and a definite aid towards good quality lighting. (The reflection factors are as assumed for kitchens.)

c. *Bedrooms*. For bedrooms a good distribution of daylight with no dark corners is more important than a high level of daylight. A minimum daylight factor of 0.5% should cover at least 60 sq ft, with the penetration not less than three-quarters the depth of room facing the window. (The reflection factors are as assumed for living rooms.)

d. *Dual purpose rooms*. Rooms which are expected to be used for more than one main purpose (e.g. kitchen–living rooms) should be lighted to the more exacting of the relevant recommendations.'

C.6   The Code also contains recommendations for educational buildings, hospitals and other sorts of buildings. Its recommendations for offices are as follows:

'*Offices*. For general office work a minimum daylight factor of 2% is recommended. This is easily achieved by top lighting. In side lit rooms, it has been customary to require a minimum daylight factor of 1% with a penetration of 12 ft from the outside wall. In practice this ensures that a substantial part of the daylight zone will be more than 2%. Exceptions to this rule are large open offices, e.g. typing pools and drawing offices. Such rooms usually demand top lighting or the supplementation of daylight by appropriately designed artificial installations.

In other offices where the visual tasks are more difficult more light is required. For example, in rooms devoted entirely to typing or the use of manually operated computers a minimum daylight factor of 4% is recommended. For the main area of use and in drawing offices, a minimum daylight factor of 6% on the drawing boards and at least 2% over the remainder of the rooms is recommended. Particular attention should be given to the direction of daylight, especially where adjustable drawing boards are to be used.'

The Building Regulations 1965

C.7   Part K of the Building Regulations contains statutory requirements regarding minimum zones of open space outside certain windows in buildings. Generally K Regulations will be much less onerous than the spacing advised in this study, but not always. In any case these zones of open space are *not* those required for adequate sunlight or daylight in the room and should not be taken as being any indication of satisfactory sunlight and daylight provision: in general they are not. The zones, trapezoidal on plan, are required outside the windows of habitable rooms. They must be unobstructed and wholly over land exclusively belonging to the building containing the window, including to the centre line of an adjacent street, etc. Where shared land occurs, it may be used in common to accommodate the required zones but no overlapping of zones to different buildings is permitted.

Building Standards (Scotland) (Consolidation) Regulations 1970

C.8   In Scotland certain regulations relating to daylight are included in the Building Standards Regulations. A table is included in Schedule 9 of these Regulations (Table 16) entitled 'Daylighting—Minimum Width of Window Openings (rooms with one window situated in the middle of the external wall).'

Rights of Light

C.9   An existing building may have statutory Rights of Light over adjoining land. It would be prudent for a prospective developer to examine the implication of any such Rights of Light for his proposals. The criteria put forward and the other matters considered in this study have no relation to statutory Rights of Light.

Index

This index gives the principal references of some subjects not specifically referred to on the *Contents* page.

Printed in England for Her Majesty's Stationery Office by
Ebenezer Baylis & Son Ltd., The Trinity Press, Worcester, and London
Dd 500576 K88 10/71